EXPERIENCING GOD WEEKEND MANUAL

Experiencing God

A Growing Disciples Weekend

LifeWay Press
Nashville, Tennessee

© Copyright 1997 • LifeWay Press
All rights reserved
Reprinted 1999, 2001

ISBN 0-7673-3879-0

This material may not be reproduced except as indicated
without the prior written permission of the publisher.

Scripture quotations are from the Holy Bible, *New International Version*,
Copyright © 1973, 1978, 1984 by International Bible Society.

Biblical pronunciations taken from *Pronouncing Bible Names*, W. Murray Severance
(Nashville: Broadman & Holman Publishers, 1994), ISBN 1-55819-418-5.

To order additional copies of this resource: WRITE LifeWay Church Resources
Customer Service, One LifeWay Plaza, Nashville, TN 37234-0113;
FAX order to (615) 251-5933; PHONE 1-800-458-2772;
EMAIL *CustomerService@lifeway.com*; order ONLINE at *www.lifeway.com*;
or visit the LifeWay Christian Store serving you.

Printed in the United States of America

Experiencing God Weekend Manual is adapted from
Experiencing God Weekend Church Preparation Manual
published by Brotherhood Commission, SBC, copyright 1993.

LifeWay Press
127 Ninth Avenue, North
Nashville, Tennessee 37234

As God works through us, we will help people and churches
know Jesus Christ and seek His kingdom by providing
biblical solutions that spiritually transform individuals and cultures.

Contents

Foreword 4

What Is an Experiencing God Weekend? 5

Experiencing God Weekend Schedule 6

Adult Section
Adult Resource Teacher 7
Visiting Small-group Leaders 16
Experiencing God Weekend Prayer Guide 18
Teaching Cels 19
Adult Participant Guide 45

Youth Section
Weekend Schedule for Youth 57
Elements of the Weekend 57
Visiting Youth Leaders 59

Children Section
Weekend Schedule for Children 60
Resource Teacher Plans 60
Children's Workbook 69
Answers to Children's Workbook 76

FOREWORD

God has initiated, and is deepening, a great hunger in the hearts of His people for a real, personal love-relationship with Himself. In the churches (leaders and members alike), is a longing to experience God. They long to know His love experientially, to know His voice practically, and to know and do His will thoroughly. Never have I seen so many people of all ages, and churches of all sizes, come to greater joy in their walk with God.

It seems that God has placed His hand of blessing upon the study, *Experiencing God: Knowing and Doing the Will of God*, which He privileged me to write along with Claude King. Our earnest prayer while writing was that it would not be just another study. We prayed (and enlisted others to pray) that this material would become an encounter with God who would change lives deeply. This has been the universal testimony of those who have used *Experiencing God* as a tool to know God.

Our continuing prayer is that "He (our Lord) must increase," and we must decrease. May God the Father, God the Son, and God the Holy Spirit become an ever-increasing reality in your life. "Jesus answered, 'I am the way and the truth and the life. No one comes to the Father except through me' " (John 14:6). May the challenge of Jesus be real as you study. " 'As the Father has loved me, so have I loved you. Now remain in my love. If you obey my commands, you will remain in my love, just as I have obeyed my Father's commands and remain in His love. I have told you this so that my joy may be in you and that your joy may be complete' " (John 15:9-11).

May our Lord be greatly honored and His people be greatly strengthened to the glory of God.

Your Friend,
Henry T. Blackaby, President
Henry Blackaby Ministries

2 Corinthians 9:8

WHAT IS AN EXPERIENCING GOD WEEKEND?

An Experiencing God Weekend exposes the church to the seven realities of how God works through His people to accomplish His purposes. Church members have the opportunity to examine their lives and seek the Lord's leadership so that they are able to join God where He is working.

The purpose of the Experiencing God Weekend is twofold. As already mentioned, a meaningful encounter with God for each participant is one major purpose. The goal of the Experiencing God Weekend is to make the seven realities personal to each participant. The other purpose is to preview the *Experiencing God: Knowing and Doing the Will of God* study to stimulate interest in individual participation in a church-wide study. Thus it is imperative that the church commit to the weekend and have a plan in mind for how the weekend will fit into the overall church plan for the 13-week study.

This manual is to be used with the *Growing Disciples Weekend Administrative Guide* (ISBN 0-7673-3859-6). Other resources for the Experiencing God Weekend and follow-up to the weekend include:

Adults
Experiencing God: Knowing and Doing the Will of God by Henry Blackaby and Claude King
(ISBN 0-8054-9954-7)
Experiencing God Leader Guide by Claude King
(ISBN 0-8054-9951-2)
The Seven Realities of Experiencing God Video Series
(ISBN 0-8054-9853-2)
Experiencing God Audiotapes (ISBN 0-7673-1927-3)
Experiencing God Videotapes (ISBN 0-7673-2776-4)
Experiencing God Bible (NKJV: ISBN 1-5581-9419-3; NIV: ISBN 1-5581-9584-X)
Experiencing God Print (ISBN 0-7673-2638-5)
When God Speaks by Henry and Richard Blackaby
(ISBN 0-8054-9822-2)

College Students
God's Invitation: A Challenge to College Students by Henry and Richard Blackaby (ISBN 0-8054-9679-3)

Youth
Experiencing God: Knowing and Doing the Will of God Youth Edition (ISBN 0-8054-9925-3)
Experiencing God Youth Edition Leader Guide
(ISBN 0-8054-9924-5)
Experiencing God Youth Edition Videos
(ISBN 0-8054-9839-7)
When God Speaks, Youth Edition by Henry and Richard Blackaby (ISBN 0-7673-2592-3)
Lift High the Torch—An Invitation to Experiencing God, Youth (ISBN 0-8054-9847-8)

Children
Experiencing God: Knowing and Doing the Will of God, Preteen Edition (ISBN 0-8054-9859-1)
Experiencing God Preteen Edition Leader Guide
(ISBN 0-8054-9860-5)
Secret Adventures Video Series (optional)

Spanish
Experiencing God Spanish Edition Adult Member Book
(ISBN 0-7673-2369-6)
Experiencing God Spanish Edition Leader Guide
(ISBN 0-7673-2370-X)
Experiencing God Spanish Bible (ISBN 1-5581-9496-7)
Experiencing God: Knowing and Doing the Will of God, Spanish Youth Edition (ISBN 0-8054-9845-1)
Experiencing God Spanish Youth Edition Leader Guide
(ISBN 0-8054-9846-X)
Experiencing God: Knowing and Doing the Will of God, Spanish Preteen Edition (ISBN 0-8054-9850-8)
Experiencing God Spanish Preteen Edition Leader Guide
(ISBN 0-8054-9851-6)

EXPERIENCING GOD WEEKEND SCHEDULE

Adjust to meet the church's needs.

Thursday
5:00 p.m.   Begin 24-hour prayer vigil

Friday
5:00 p.m.   Team meeting
6:00 p.m.   Churchwide fellowship meal
6:45 p.m.   General session for everyone
                     Music and testimonies
7:30 p.m.*   Adult Teaching Session #1:
                     Introduction and Reality 1
8:15 p.m.*   Adult small-group discussions
9:15 p.m.   Reconvene for closing praise time
                     Pair hosts and guests

Saturday
8:00 a.m.   Team meeting
9:00 a.m.*   General session for adults
                     Music and testimonies
9:10 a.m.*   Adult Teaching Session #2:
                     Realities 2 and 3
10:15 a.m.*   Break
10:30 a.m.*   Adult Teaching Session #3:
                     Realities 4 and 5
11:30 a.m.   Testimonies and prayer time
12:15 p.m.   Lunch
                     (Option: Lunch can be omitted and
                     the small-group discussions take
                     place from 11:30 a.m. to 12:30 p.m.
                     Everyone is dismissed at 12:30 for
                     the afternoon.)
1:00 p.m.*   Adult small-group discussions
2:00 p.m.   Dismiss for the afternoon
5:00 p.m.   Team meeting
6:00 p.m.   Churchwide fellowship meal
6:45 p.m.   General session for everyone
                     Music and testimonies

7:30 p.m.*   Adult Teaching Session #4:
                     Realities 6 and 7
8:15 p.m.*   Small-group discussions
9:00 p.m.*   Reconvene for adult small-group
                     commitment time

Sunday
8:15 a.m.   Team meeting
9:30 a.m.   Sunday School (adults and youth
                     meet together)
10:45 a.m.   Worship service
                     Testimonies and commitment time
12:30 p.m.   Lunch for visiting team members
6:00 p.m.   Evaluation time: What is God
                     saying to you?
                     Commitment to *Experiencing God:*
                     Knowing and Doing the Will of God

*Youth and children meet separately with their resource teachers. See Weekend Schedule for Youth (p. 57) and Weekend Schedule for Children (p. 60) for their specific schedules.

ADULT SECTION

ADULT RESOURCE TEACHER

As the resource teacher, remember that the strongest reinforcement of the seven realities will be the Scripture and personal testimonies from visiting team members who have been through *Experiencing God: Knowing and Doing the Will of God*.

Guidelines for Adult Resource Teachers

- Complete *Experiencing God: Knowing and Doing the Will of God* at least once and if possible lead a group through it.
- Work through the teaching session plans that follow and the Adult Participant Guide beginning on page 45 in this manual.
- Remember that you are introducing the study. Don't teach the total content. Deal with the seven realities and the personal application.
- Make it personal. Get it in your heart before you attempt to teach it. Use visiting team members to share testimonies about each reality.
- Stay with the time frame for each teaching session. The personal testimonies from visiting team members and the small-group discussions will reinforce your teaching.
- Work closely with the weekend coordinator before and during the weekend.
- Know the direction each session is taking. Each session builds on the previous session.
- Be prepared to do the total review of all seven realities in about 45 minutes during the Sunday School hour. Remember that seven testimonies from visiting team members are included in the 45-minute time frame.
- Read the summary statements of each unit in *Experiencing God: Knowing and Doing the Will of God* as a review of the key thoughts.
- Use the overhead cels to introduce the main point of each reality.
- Continually evaluate the weekend. Ask for comments from the pastor and church staff, church members, and visiting team members.
- Keep the study simple and understandable.

The following material is provided as a guide to help you teach during the weekend. Include as many personal experiences as possible. Stay within the time frame. Cover the material that corresponds to the Adult Participant Guide and keep the focus clear in each teaching session. The following material is in script form; ideas in parenthesis are further instructions.

Teaching Session 1 (Friday, 7:30-8:15 p.m.)

INTRODUCTION

Most people who have been involved with a church for long have certain perceptions about God, church, and the Bible. Much of what we perceive is wrong. We've complicated the Christian life and made it something mechanical, not what God had in mind. We need to get back to some basics.

DISPLAY CEL 1

(Call attention to page 1 of the Adult Participant Guide and encourage participants to fill in the blanks and take additional notes as God speaks through the session.)

1. *The Bible is your guide for faith and practice.*

The Bible is God's Word to you. The Bible is your source of authority as you listen to identify where God is at work. Every time you sense God working in a certain area, it must always line up with what Scripture says. God never works in a situation that is contrary to His Word.

The Holy Spirit is your personal teacher. He is the One who guides you to hear the voice of God through the Word of God and how it applies to your life.

2. *Jesus is your way.*

(Share the illustration about the map on page 10 of *Experiencing God: Knowing and Doing the Will of God* or an illustration from your own experience about Jesus being the map for your life.)

When you come to the Lord Jesus to seek His will for your life, which of the following requests is most like what you say to Him?

"Lord, what do You want me to do? When do You want me to do it? How shall I do it? Where shall I do it? Who do You want me to involve along the way? And please tell me what the outcome will be."

Or do you say,

"Lord, just tell me what to do one step at a time, and I will do it."

Isn't the first response most typical of us? We ask God for a detailed road map. We say, "Lord, if You could just tell me where I am heading, then I will be able to set my course and go."

God says, "You don't need to know. You need to follow Me one day at a time." We need to learn to respond to Him like that every day.

Jesus said, "I am the Way." He wants us to learn to hear Him speak and to know where He is working and become involved there. Christ wants us to be His servants.

What does that mean to you? (Allow participants to respond before proceeding.)

3. *To be a servant of God you must be moldable and remain in the hand of the Master.*

(Share the lesson of the potter and the clay found on page 16 of *Experiencing God: Knowing and Doing the Will of God.*)

Let's remember that ...

- A servant is always under construction, being molded by the Master.
- A servant remains tuned in to the Master on a daily basis so God can use him or her any way He chooses. Since God made the servant, He knows best how to use him or her.

4. *To know God, you must experience Him.*

John 17:3 says, "This is eternal life: that they may know you, the only true God, and Jesus Christ, whom you have sent." (Read from the Amplified Version if you have one.)

In order to have eternal life we must know God and know Jesus Christ whom God sent. Knowing God doesn't happen through a program or a method. It happens when we have a relationship with Him. It is an intimate, loving relationship where God tells us what's on His heart and we hear Him and join Him in His heart-concerns. We cease being self-centered and become God-centered. When we obey Him, God does things through us that only He can do. That's when we know God in a more intimate way—by experiencing God at work through us.

The study *Experiencing God: Knowing and Doing the Will of God* will help you move into that kind of intimate relationship with God. Jesus said in John 10:10, "I have come that they may have life, and have it to the full." You can experience life to the full if you are willing to respond to God's invitation to an intimate love relationship with Him.

5. *God is love. His will is always best.*

As you begin to experience God, you learn that God is love. His will is always best.

(Read the following Scripture references to support this truth: Psalm 139:1-6, Psalm 37:23-24, and Proverbs 20:24.)

We must remember that God desires to build our character and make us more like Jesus. Everything in our lives happens because God loves us and He wants to use each situation to mold us into His image. God cannot make a mistake because ... (move into the next point) ...

6. *God is all-knowing. His directions are always right.*

God knows everything. He understands things we could never understand. God sees things we can't see. And God always directs our steps in the right ways because of His all-knowing nature.

7. *God is all-powerful. He can enable you to do His will.*

When we come to believe that God's will is always best and right, then He will demonstrate His power. God can enable us to do His will.

Philippians 2:13 says, "It is God who works in you to will and to act according to his good purpose." We need to recognize that what God has worked in us is His will for us. It is something different for each of us, but it is perfect. God is love and His will is always best. If God has been in

the process of molding us for His use, we can confidently proclaim Philippians 4:13: "I can do everything through him who gives me strength."

REALITY 1
God is always at work around you.

(Instruct participants to turn to page 2 in the Adult Participant Guide. Ask the designated visiting team member to give his or her testimony related to Reality 1.)

DISPLAY CEL 2
(Read John 5:17,19-20)
  (Ask the following questions and allow time for participants to answer. Be conscious of the time remaining. Encourage note taking.)
  • According to John 5:17, who is always at work? (God, the Father)
  • How much can the Son do by Himself? (Nothing)
  • What does the Son do? (Only what He sees His Father doing)
  • Why does the Father show the Son what He is doing? (The Father loves the Son)

Right now God is working all around you and in your life. All through the Bible we see that God has been involved in the world from the beginning of time. And God always takes the initiative and involves His people in His work. God chooses to work through people to accomplish His purposes.

When God was ready to judge the world, He came to Noah.

When God was ready to build a nation for Himself, He came to Abraham.

When God heard the cry of the children of Israel and decided to deliver them, He appeared to Moses.

Look at the example of Jesus in John 5:
• The Father has been working right up to now.
• Now God has Me working.
• I do nothing on My own initiative.
• I do what I see the Father already is doing.
• The Father loves Me.
• He shows me everything that He, Himself, is doing.

It's easy to see God at work in the Bible and through Jesus' example, but what about in our own lives? Most often, even though we desire to experience God, we don't realize that He is working every day and we aren't able to recognize Him.

Experiencing God: Knowing and Doing the Will of God will help you learn ways to recognize clearly the activity of God in and around you. Once you begin to recognize God working around you, you will learn how to adjust your life and join Him in His work.

John 12:26 says, "Whoever serves me must follow me; and where I am, my servant also will be. My Father will honor the one who serves me."

How do we do this?

DISPLAY CEL 3
1. Find out where the Master is, then that is where you need to be.
2. Watch to see where God is working and join Him. This is not a step-by-step approach for knowing God's will. This describes a love relationship through which God accomplishes His purposes through those who love Him.
3. The right question is: What is God's will? People often ask, "What is God's will for my life?" Is that the right question? Henry Blackaby says it's not. The right question is "What is God's will?" Once you know God's will, you can adjust your life to Him. Once you know what God is doing where you are, then you can know what you should be doing. The focus needs to shift from your life to God.

God's will is what you would do if you knew all the facts. God's work is what Jesus would do in your place. Remember Reality 1: God is always at work around you.

Teaching Session 2 (Saturday, 9:10-10:15 a.m.)

INTRODUCTION
Remember Reality 1: God is always at work around you. In this session we continue with Reality 2.

REALITY 2
God pursues a continuing love relationship with you that is real and personal.

(Ask the designated visiting team member to give his or her testimony related to Reality 2.)

DISPLAY CEL 4 FOLLOWED BY CEL 5
(Go through cels 4 and 5 using personal comments to illustrate the points.)

How does God build our character to match the assignment? Here's how:

DISPLAY CEL 6
Every assignment God gives you is a new venture of faith. You know Him, love Him, believe Him, trust Him, and obey Him, so that you can turn right back around and know Him, love Him, believe Him, trust Him, and obey Him for the next assignment. God pursues a continuing love relationship with you that is real and personal.

(Invite participants to turn to page 4 in the Adult Participant Guide. Instruct them to form groups of three and work together through "A Love Relationship." Give them 8 to 10 minutes. At the end of that time, ask groups to share their responses.)

This leads us to Reality 3.

REALITY 3
God invites you to become involved with Him in His work.

DISPLAY CEL 7
(Ask the designated visiting team member to give his or her testimony related to Reality 3.)

The Bible is not primarily a book about individual persons and their relationship with God. It is about the activity of God and His relationship with individuals. The Bible is the record of God's activity in the world. In it God reveals Himself (His nature), His purposes and plans, and His ways. The focus is on God and His activity.

Two factors are important for you to be able to recognize the activity of God around you:

1. You must be living in an intimate love relationship with God.
2. God must take the initiative to open your spiritual eyes so you can see what He is doing.

Unless God allows you to see where He is working, you will not see it. Recognizing God's activity is dependent upon your love relationship with Him and His taking the initiative to open your spiritual eyes to it. Consider these principles.

• You never find God asking persons to dream up what they want to do for Him. He takes the initiative. When God is about to do something, He takes the initiative and comes to one or more of His servants. God lets them know what He is about to do. God invites them to adjust their lives to Him, so He can accomplish His work through them. Amos 3:7 says, "The Sovereign Lord does nothing without revealing His plan to His servants the prophets."

• Understanding what God is about to do where you are is more important than telling God what you want to do for Him. God is in control. The issue is whether you have acknowledged that and given Him control of your life. God never follows. He always leads.

• God's revelation of His activity is an invitation for you to join Him. You may be asking, "How does God invite me to be involved with Him?" Go back to page 1 in your guide and look again at Jesus' example in John 5:17,19-20. (Briefly review the section on Jesus' example, Cel 2.)

How did Jesus know what to do in His Father's work? How did He respond? Jesus said He watched to see what the Father was doing. Then He (Jesus) joined him (God) in that work.

The key word in the fourth statement is "watch." Jesus watched the Father to see what He was doing. When you see the Father at work around you, that is your invitation to adjust your life to Him and join Him in that work.

• You cannot know the activity of God unless He takes the initiative to reveal it to you. When God reveals what He is doing, that is the time for you to respond. God speaks when He is ready to accomplish His purpose. That is true throughout Scripture. Remember, though, that the final completion may be a long time off. Abram's son was born 25 years after the promise from God. The time God comes to you and reveals where He is working, however, is the time for you to respond. You need to begin adjusting your life to Him. You may need to make some changes in your plans. You may need to rearrange your calendar or even your life.

Isaiah 46:11 states: "What I have said, that will I bring about; what I have planned, that will I do."

And Isaiah 14:24,27 states:
The Lord Almighty has sworn,
"Surely, as I have planned, so it will be,
    and as I have purposed, so it will stand."
... For the Lord Almighty has purposed,
    and who can thwart Him?
His hand is stretched out, and who
    can turn it back?

God says that when He lets His people know what He is doing it is as good as done. God Himself will bring it to pass.

What God speaks, He guarantees that it will come to pass. This holds enormous implications to individual believers, churches, and denominations. When you come to God, to know what He is about to do where you are, you also come with the assurance that what God indicates He is about to do is certain to come to pass. It may be necessary to remind ourselves often of His promise in Philippians 1:6: "He who began a good work in you will carry it on to completion until the day of Christ Jesus."

• There are some things that only God can do. When you see one of these things happening you can know God is at work.

DISPLAY CEL 8

There are some things only God can do:
    God draws people to Himself.
    God causes people to seek after Him.
    God reveals spiritual truth.
    God convicts the world of guilt regarding sin.
    God convicts the world of righteousness.
    God convicts the world of judgment.

When you see one or more of these things happening you know God is at work. When you see someone coming to faith in Christ, asking about spiritual matters, coming to understand spiritual truths, being convicted of sin, being convinced of the righteousness of Christ and of the coming judgment, God is at work. Begin adjusting your life so that you can join Him at that place.

Consider the incident of Jesus and Zacchaeus. As Jesus passed through a crowd, He was always looking for where the Father was at work. The crowd was not the harvest field. The harvest field was somewhere within that crowd. Jesus saw Zacchaeus in a tree. He knew Zacchaeus had gone the extra mile to see Jesus and must have been really seeking Him. So Jesus left the crowd and concentrated on Zacchaeus. Jesus said, "Zacchaeus, come down here. I'd like to spend some time with you."

What happened? Salvation came to Zacchaeus that night.

Jesus was always looking for signs of the activity of God around Him and then joining the Father.

(If time permits, share the story of the college campus Bible studies on page 26 of *Experiencing God: Knowing and Doing the Will of God*.)

DISPLAY CEL 9

(Encourage participants to fill in the blanks as you review the six principles. Answer any questions.)

Dismiss for a break before the next session.

Teaching Session 3 (Saturday, 10:30-11:30 a.m.)

INTRODUCTION

Let's review the first three realities.
Reality 1: God is always at work around you.
Reality 2: God pursues a continuing love relationship with you that is real and personal.
Reality 3: God invites you to become involved with Him in His work.
In this session we continue with Reality 4.

REALITY 4

God speaks by the Holy Spirit through the Bible, prayer, circumstances, and the church to reveal Himself, His purposes, and His ways.

(Ask the designated visiting team member to give his or her testimony related to Reality 4.)

DISPLAY CEL 10

" 'He who belongs to God hears what God says. The reason you do not hear is that you do not belong to God' " (John 8:47).

Keep in mind that hearing God speak is dependent upon our love relationship with Him. Turn to page 7 in your Adult Participant Guide and let's look closer at Reality 4.

1. *In the Old Testament God spoke in many ways. That God spoke is the most important factor, not how He spoke.*

    a. *When God spoke, it was usually unique to that individual.* For instance, Moses had no precedent for a burning-bush experience. He couldn't say, "Oh, this is my burning-bush experience. My fathers, Abraham, Isaac, and Jacob had their burning bushes, and this is mine." There were no other examples of God speaking this way. It was unique, because God wants our experience with Him to be unique to us. He wants us to look to Him rather than depend on some method or technique. If Moses were alive today, he would probably be tempted to write a book entitled, *My Burning Bush Experience.* Then people all over the world would be trying to find a bush like Moses'. The important thing is not how God spoke, but that He spoke. That has not changed. God still speaks to His people today.

    b. *When God spoke, the person was sure God was speaking.* Because God spoke to Moses in a unique way, Moses had to be certain it was God. Scripture says that Moses knew immediately that "I AM" was speaking with him. Could Moses logically prove to someone else that he had heard from God? No. All Moses could do was testify to his encounter with God. Only God could cause His people to know that the word He gave Moses was a word from the God of their fathers.

    c. *When God spoke, the person knew what God said.* Moses knew what God was telling him to do. He knew how God wanted to work through him. That is why Moses raised so many objections. Moses knew exactly what God was expecting. This was his time of crisis of belief.

    d. *When God spoke, that was the encounter with God.* Moses would have been foolish to say, "This has been a wonderful experience with this burning bush. I hope this leads me to an encounter with God." That *was* the encounter with God. When God reveals truth to you, by whatever means, it is an experience of His presence in your life.

DISPLAY CEL 11

2. *In the Gospels God spoke by His Son.* (Ask someone to read Hebrews 1:1-2.)
3. *In Acts and to the present God speaks by the Holy Spirit.* (Ask someone to read John 14:26 and 16:13-14.)
4. *Knowing God's voice comes from an intimate love relationship with Him.* If you want to know the will and voice of God, you must give the time and effort to cultivate a love relationship with Him.
5. *God speaks when He has a purpose in mind for your life.*
6. *The moment God speaks to you is God's timing.*

DISPLAY CEL 12

7. *You never discover truth. Truth is revealed.* Sometimes we do not hear God because our love relationship with Him is lacking. We may need a spiritual tune-up. (Ask someone to read John 8:47.)
8. *God reveals Himself to increase your faith.* God reveals Himself to increase faith that leads to action. You need to listen attentively to what God reveals to you about Himself. This will be critical when you come to the crisis of belief.
    * You have to believe God is who He says He is.
    * You have to believe God can do what He says He will do.
    * You have to adjust your thinking in light of this belief.
    * Trusting that God will demonstrate Himself to be who He says He is, you then obey Him.
    * When you obey, God does His work through you and demonstrates that He is who He says He is.
    * Then you will know God by experience.
    * You will know God is who He says He is.
9. *God reveals His purposes so you will do His work.* What you plan to do for God is not important. What He plans to do where you are is very important. God speaks with a purpose in mind. When God came to Noah, He did not ask, "What do you

want to do for me?" He came to reveal what He was about to do. It was far more important to know what God was about to do. God was about to destroy the world and He wanted to work through Noah to accomplish His purpose of saving a remnant of people and animals to repopulate the earth.

10. *God reveals His ways so you can accomplish His purposes.* God's goal always is to reveal Himself to people to draw them into a love relationship with Himself. God's ways are redemptive. He acts in such a way as to reveal Himself and His love. God does not simply wait around in order to help you achieve your goals for Him. God comes to accomplish His goals through you—and in His own way.

God's purposes accomplished in His ways bring glory to Him. You must learn to do kingdom work in kingdom ways.

During the study of *Experiencing God: Knowing and Doing the Will of God* you will learn how God also speaks through the Bible, prayer, circumstances, and the church to reveal Himself, His purposes, and His ways.

DISPLAY CEL 13 FOLLOWED BY 14 AND 15.

(Briefly explain each cel. If you need additional material, check Units 5 and 6 of *Experiencing God: Knowing and Doing the Will of God.*)

Now we come to a critical point in the process.

REALITY 5

God's invitation for you to work with Him always leads you to a crisis of belief that requires faith and action.

(Ask the designated visiting team member to give his or her testimony related to Reality 5.)

DISPLAY CEL 16

(Invite the group turn to page 8 in the Adult Participant Guide and answer questions 1-3 based on the Scriptures on the cel.)

DISPLAY CEL 17

When God reveals His activity in a situation it creates a crisis of belief. In a crisis of belief you have to make a decision about what you really believe about God. It is a turning point in your life.

We know that without faith it is impossible to please God. An encounter with God requires faith and action. Sometimes the action required can't be explained by common sense. Encounters with God are always God-sized, not man-sized. Our world is not seeing God because we are not attempting anything that only God can do. What we do in response to God's revelation (invitation) reveals what we believe about God. Faith is a Person. Faith in God always requires action of some kind.

DISPLAY CEL 18

(Be prepared to share at least one of the examples on the cel. Invite the group to turn in their Bibles to the reference and follow along. Encourage them to take notes as you illustrate a crisis of belief.)

Where does God have you right now? What is He doing in your life?

(Close the session in prayer.)

Teaching Session 4 (Saturday, 7:30-8:15 p.m.)
Time to review the first five realities.
Reality 1: God is always at work around you.
Reality 2: God pursues a continuing love relationship with you that is real and personal.
Reality 3: God invites you to become involved with Him in His work.
Reality 4: God speaks by the Holy Spirit through the Bible, prayer, circumstances, and the church to reveal Himself, His purposes, and His ways.
Reality 5: God's invitation for you to work with Him always leads you to a crisis of belief that requires faith and action.

In this final session we will look at Realities 6 and 7.

REALITY 6
You must make major adjustments in your life to join God in what He is doing.

God never works the same way in two people's lives. However, there are some common points that can be identified when God is working in people's lives.

Luke 14:33 says, "Any of you who does not give up everything he has cannot be my disciple."

That verse states certain truths about following God.

DISPLAY CEL 19 FOLLOWED BY CEL 20
(Refer participants to page 9 in the Adult Participant Guide. Work through the nine points on the two cels. Ask participants to add names to the lists of examples and non-examples.)

(Ask the designated visiting team member to give his or her testimony related to Reality 6.)

DISPLAY CEL 21
(Talk about the kinds of adjustments that may be necessary using experiences from your own life to illustrate. Include at least one testimony from a group member about adjustments he or she has made in experiencing God.)

REALITY 7
You come to know God by experience as you obey Him and He accomplishes His work through you.

DISPLAY CEL 22
John 14:15,21,23-24 says:
"If you love me, you will obey what I command. Whoever has my commands and obeys them, he is the one who loves me. He who loves me will be loved by my Father, and I too will love him and show myself to him. If anyone loves me, he will obey my teaching. My Father will love him, and we will come to him and make our home with him. He who does not love me will not obey my teaching."

(Ask the designated visiting team member to give his or her testimony related to Reality 7.)

DISPLAY CEL 23
(Briefly share the following eight points. Encourage the group to fill in the blanks and take notes on page 11 in their Adult Participant Guide.)

1. *Obey what you already know to be God's will. Obey His commands.*
2. *Affirmation comes after obedience.* (Read Exodus 3:12.)
3. *Obedience is the outward expression of your love of God.*
4. *Disobedience is costly. God does not always give second chances.* (Briefly reference the experiences of Nadab and Abihu in Leviticus 10 and Jonah.)
5. *If you have an obedience problem, you have a love problem.*
6. *If you love God, you will obey Him.*
7. *The reward for obedience and love is that He will reveal Himself to you.* (Read John 14:21,23.)

DISPLAY CEL 24
8. *God reveals Himself to His people by what He does.* (Read the examples on Cel 24; if time allows, read two or three of the Scripture references.)

(Have a testimony from a visiting team member about one or more of these points.)

In closing, let's review the seven realities of experiencing God.

DISPLAY CEL 25
(Review Cel 25. Close with an invitation to Sunday's activities. Pray God will work in the lives of participants throughout the remainder of the weekend.)

Sunday School

You will need to provide an overview of the seven realities during the regular Sunday School time. Adults and youth will be meeting together. Some of them will not have attended previous weekend activities. It is for these people that you will need to be clear and precise in your presentation. For those who have attended all weekend, this will be a time of review and reflection.

Make handouts of Cels 25 and 26 to distribute during Sunday School. Using these two cels, have one or more team members give a brief personal testimony on each reality. Be sure that the team member(s) understands that his or her testimony needs to explain clearly each reality.

Make any necessary comments to further clarify the reality.

Morning Worship

As you prepare for the weekend, be sensitive to what God is saying to you personally. Sunday morning's sermon should be an overflow from your experience with God. Your message should be a fresh word from God. The desired outcome of the message is that the congregation will see how the seven realities apply to the body of believers.

Stay within the time frame for the Sunday morning service. The invitation should begin on time. If you sense the Holy Spirit moving during the invitation in an unusual way, explain that those who need to leave should feel free to do so. With the pastor's permission, extend the invitation as long as he senses appropriate.

VISITING SMALL-GROUP LEADERS

Correspondence and Materials Group: The following pages should be duplicated and mailed to the visiting adult small-group leaders as you receive their confirmation cards.

Facilitating a small group can be a rewarding experience. This may be the first time you have led a small group. To make the small group more effective, consider the following suggestions.
1. You are a facilitator. That means you do not teach the material; you lead an open discussion of the material shared during the teaching sessions.
2. You will be asking questions to motivate open discussion among your small group. When you ask a question, don't be afraid of silence. Allow time for them to think and formulate a reply. Don't panic and feel that you have to fill the silence. If after a minute or two no one responds, call on an outgoing person for their thoughts. Be prepared to help participants verbalize their thoughts, but don't fall into the trap of answering for them.
3. Ninety percent of your time should be spent in listening to your group.
4. Learn how to deal with the one or two individuals who will tend to dominate the discussion. If there are people like that in your group, listen for a pause and then say, "That's a good observation. What do the rest of you think about that?" Usually someone else will be ready to join the conversation. If not, go on to the next question.
5. You aren't expected to have all the answers. Sometimes it will put the group at ease if you ask, What do you think? Most groups respond best when there is an openness from the leader. Don't be afraid to be vulnerable.
6. When a person expresses a personal need or concern, stop at that point and minister to that person. God has put you there to meet that need as a group. Ask for a volunteer to pray for the person and their need. Allow enough time for the Lord to minister through you and the group. A person's need is God's first priority.

For more information on small groups, read *Journey Into Small Groups* by William Bangham.

Friday Evening Small-group Discussion
Teaching Session 1 introduces the weekend and covers Reality 1 of experiencing God. Put the group at ease by having everyone introduce themselves. Ask if they have had the opportunity to study *Experiencing God: Knowing and Doing the Will of God*.

Tell the group that during the small-group discussions they need only to participate as the Holy Spirit leads and as they feel comfortable.

Pose the following questions and allow ample time for response.
- What does "experiencing God" mean to you?"
- What is your impression of tonight's session?
- Which of the seven realities are you most interested in learning about? Why?
- What do you see God doing in your church?
- What do you see God doing in your life? In your family?
- Has God said anything specific to you tonight? Would you share this with the group?
- What do you sense you need to do to join God in His work around you or your church?

Close the small-group discussion with conversational prayer and return to the worship center.

Saturday Morning Small-group Discussion
Teaching Session 2 covers Realities 2 and 3. Teaching Session 3 covers Realities 4 and 5. The small-group discussion comes at the end of the morning. Invite members to introduce themselves. Remind the group that they should feel free to join in as the Holy Spirit leads. Pray for individual needs and requests as they come up during the discussion.

Ask if anyone would like to share something God impressed upon them this morning. The response may help you choose the next question.

- Reality 2 says *God pursues a continuing love relationship with you that is real and personal.* Has God revealed His love for you in a special way? Would you share it with our group?
- Reality 3 says *God invites you to become involved with Him in His work.* Has there ever been a time in your life when God invited you to join Him in His work? How did you respond?
- Reality 4 says *God speaks by the Holy Spirit through the Bible, prayer, circumstances, and the church to reveal Himself, His purposes, and His ways.* Has God ever spoken to you in a special way? If so, would you share it and tell us how He spoke to you (prayer, circumstances, Bible, other Christians)?
- Reality 5 says *God's invitation for you to work with Him always leads you to a crisis of belief that requires faith and action.* Although you might not have thought of it in those terms before, when did you experience a crisis of belief?
- Do you see things God is doing in this church or in the lives of your friends, family, or yourself that you did not see before today?
- What do we as a church, or you as an individual, need to do to respond to what God is revealing to us this weekend?

Close with conversational prayer. Remind the group of tonight's schedule.

Saturday Evening Small-group Discussion
Teaching Session 4 covers Realities 6 and 7. Break the ice with quick introductions and remind the group to join in as they feel led by the Holy Spirit.

Explain that tonight they will try to determine what God has been doing in their lives.

Ask them to react to this statement: "You come to know God as you obey Him and He accomplishes His work through you."

Use the analogy to secular friendship: true friendship is based on shared experiences over a period of time. Discuss that concept as it applies to a relationship with God.

Ask, Has there ever been a time when you had to make a major adjustment so God could work through you? If so, what happened as a result?

Remind your small-group members that God is more interested in their love relationship with Him and with developing their character than He is with the things they do for Him. God often develops character through the events in their lives.

Explain that there are usually times in our lives when we are sure God has guided us in a decision, given us direction, or been with us through a significant experience. These times are "spiritual markers." Like a road map, these significant times form a pattern that gives us some idea of what God has been, and is doing in our lives. And like a road map, we can often get an indication of where we are going from where we have been and the road we are on.

Have the participants turn to page 12 in their Adult Participant Guide. Allow 15 minutes for them to complete the Spiritual Markers Worksheet. Remind them that what they write down is between them and the Lord. Leaders should also do this exercise. Before they begin, lead the group in prayer asking God to reveal to them their spiritual markers and what adjustments need to be made so they can obey God and allow Him to work in their lives.

After 15 minutes, invite the group to the worship center for a time of prayer and commitment. Remind them that there may be others praying as they enter. Suggest that when they finish they should pick up their children and move somewhere else if they plan to fellowship.

Lead the group to the worship center. Form a circle of prayer. Tell them that you will begin and end the prayer. Invite those who would like to pray out loud to pray about the adjustments and commitments the Lord is leading them to make. When the prayer time concludes, remind them that there will be visiting team members around to talk and pray with them.

Sunday Morning Responsibilities
All adults and youth meet together for Sunday School. Though your small group does not meet together, you need to be present through the morning worship service to assist the weekend coordinator and be available for counseling.

EXPERIENCING GOD WEEKEND PRAYER GUIDE

Correspondence and Materials Group: This page should be printed in church publications or duplicated and mailed to church members as a tool for spiritual preparation for the weekend.

This guide will help you pray for the Experiencing God Weekend to be held in our church on …

_____
(date)

Remember, prayer is a relationship, not just a religious activity. Each of the seven realities of God are shared in the seven days of prayer leading to the weekend. Are you ready for a God-sized assignment? Pray, watch, and seek because God is ready to do something special in your life. Each day pray for:

- visiting leaders for the weekend
- the 24-hour prayer vigil
- our pastor
- God's cleansing in your life
- God's direction for our church
- our church staff
- the weekend participants

Day 1
Reality 1: God is always at work around you.
Read Jeremiah 18:1-6. To know and do the will of God, I must deny self and return to a God-centered life. I must become clay in God's hands, then He will mold me for His work.

Day 2
Reality 2: God pursues a continuing love relationship with you that is real and personal.
Read Matthew 22:37-38. A love relationship with God is more important than any other factor in life. I must do my part to maintain this love relationship with God.

Day 3
Reality 3: God invites you to become involved with Him in His work.
Read John 14:21. If I love Him, I will obey Him. When I see the Father at work around me, that is my invitation to adjust my life to Him and join Him in that work.

Day 4
Reality 4: God speaks by the Holy Spirit through the Bible, prayer, circumstances, and the church to reveal Himself, His purposes, and His ways.
Read John 8:47. God has not changed. He still speaks to His people. I understand spiritual truth, because the Holy Spirit is working in my life.

Day 5
Reality 5: God's invitation for you to work with Him always leads you to a crisis of belief that requires faith and action.
Read Hebrews 11:6. How I live my life is a testimony of what I believe about God. Our world is not seeing God because we are not attempting anything that only God can do.

Day 6
Reality 6: You must make major adjustments in your life to join God in what He is doing.
Read Luke 14:33. Obedience will be costly to me and those around me, but I can trust God with my family and my life.

Day 7
Reality 7: You come to know God by experience as you obey Him and He accomplishes His work through you.
Read John 14:23. God will never give me an assignment that He will not enable me to complete. God, what are you calling me to do?

EXPERIENCING GOD
Knowing and Doing the Will of God

1. The Bible is your guide for faith and practice.

2. Jesus is your way.

3. To be a servant of God you must be moldable and remain in the hand of the Master.

4. To know God, you must experience Him.

5. God is love. His will is always best.

6. God is all-knowing. His directions are always right.

7. God is all-powerful. He can enable you to do His will.

REALITY 1
God is always at work around you.

" 'My Father is always at his work to this very day, and I, too, am working. I tell you the truth, the Son can do nothing by himself; he can do only what he sees his Father doing, because whatever the Father does the Son also does. For the Father loves the Son and shows him all he does' " (John 5:17,19-20).

Jesus' Example
- The Father has been working right up to now.
- Now God has Me working.
- I do nothing on My own initiative.
- I do what I see the Father already is doing.
- The Father loves me.
- He shows me everything that He, Himself, is doing.

REALITY 1
(continued)

How Do We Follow and Serve God?

1. Find out where the Master is, then that is where you need to be.

2. Watch to see where God is working and join Him.

3. The right question is: What is God's will?

REALITY 2
God pursues a continuing love relationship with you that is real and personal.

God pursues ...

The Lord appeared to us in the past saying:

"I have loved you with an everlasting love;

I have drawn you with loving-kindness" (Jeremiah 31:3).

... a love relationship

"Love the Lord your God with all your heart and with all your soul and with all your mind. This is the first and greatest commandment" (Matthew 22:37-38).

Can you describe your relationship with God by sincerely saying, "I love you with all my heart"?

- Everything in your Christian life, everything about knowing Him and experiencing Him, everything about knowing His will, depends on the quality of your love relationship.

REALITY 2
(continued)

- A love relationship with God is more important than any other single factor in your life.

- God created you for a love relationship that is real and personal.

- The constant presence of God is the most practical part of your life and ministry.

- God created you not for time but for eternity.

- Let your present be molded and shaped by what you are to become in Christ, not by your past.

- Your character is more important to God than what you do. God develops character to match the assignment.

LOVE RELATIONSHIP WITH GOD

Know Him

Love Him

Believe Him

Trust Him

Obey Him

We are called to a love relationship before we are called to any form of ministry or service. The quality of my love relationship will determine the effectiveness of any kind of ministry.

Love Relationship = Usefulness to God

REALITY 3

God invites you to become involved with Him in His work.

- You never find God asking persons to dream up what they want to do for Him. He takes the initiative.

- Understanding what God is about to do where you are is more important than telling God what you want to do for Him.

- God's revelation of His activity is an invitation for you to join Him.

- You cannot know the activity of God unless He takes the initiative to reveal it to you.

- There are some things that only God can do. When you see one of these things happening, you can know God is at work.

REALITY 3
(continued)

Things Only God Can Do

- God draws people to Himself.

- God causes people to seek after Him.

- God reveals spiritual truth.

- God convicts the world of guilt regarding sin.

- God convicts the world of righteousness.

- God convicts the world of judgment.

REALITY 3
(continued)

When you want to know what God is doing around you:

1. Pray and watch to see what God does next.

2. Make the connection between your prayer and what happens next.

3. Find out what God is already doing.

4. Ask probing questions …
   - How can I pray for you?
   - What can I pray for you?
   - Do you want to talk?
   - What do you see as the greatest challenge in your life?
   - What is the most significant thing happening in your life right now?
   - Would you tell me what God is doing in your life?
   - What is God bringing to the surface in your life?
   - What particular burden has God given you?

5. Listen.

6. Be ready to make the necessary adjustments in order to join God in what He is doing.

REALITY 4
God speaks by the Holy Spirit through the Bible, prayer, circumstances, and the church to reveal Himself, His purposes, and His ways.

" 'He who belongs to God hears what God says. The reason you do not hear is that you do not belong to God' " (John 8:47).

1. In the Old Testament God spoke in many ways. That God spoke is the most important factor, not how He spoke.

    a. When God spoke, it was usually unique to that individual.

    b. When God spoke, the person was sure God was speaking.

    c. When God spoke, the person knew what God said.

    d. When God spoke, that was the encounter with God.

REALITY 4
(continued)

2. In the Gospels God spoke by His Son.

3. In Acts and to the present God speaks by the Holy Spirit.

4. Knowing God's voice comes from an intimate love relationship with Him.

5. God speaks when He has a purpose in mind for your life.

6. The moment God speaks to you is God's timing.

REALITY 4
(continued)

7. You never discover truth. Truth is revealed.

8. God reveals Himself to increase your faith.

9. God reveals His purposes so you will do His work.

10. God reveals His ways so you can accomplish His purposes.

REALITY 4
(continued)

God Speaks Through the Bible

REALITY 4
(continued)

God Speaks Through Prayer

REALITY 4
(continued)

God Speaks Through Circumstances

REALITY 5

God's invitation for you to work with Him always leads you to a crisis of belief that requires faith and action.

"Without faith it is impossible to please God, because anyone who comes to him must believe that he exists and that he rewards those who earnestly seek him" (Hebrews 11:6).

"Faith is being sure of what we hope for and certain of what we do not see" (Hebrews 11:1).

"We live by faith, not by sight" (2 Corinthians 5:7).

REALITY 5
(continued)

- The crisis of belief is a turning point where you must make a decision. You must decide what you really believe about God.

- An encounter with God requires faith and action.

- Encounters with God are God-sized.

- Our world is not seeing God because we are not attempting anything that only God can do.

- What you do in response to God's revelation (invitation) reveals what you believe about God.

- Faith is in a Person.

- True faith requires action.

REALITY 5
(continued)

Examples of a Crisis of Belief

• Joshua and the walls of Jericho (Joshua 6:1-5)

• Gideon (Judges 6:33; 7:1-8)

• David and the Philistines (1 Chronicles 14:8-6)

• Peter, a fish, and taxes (Matthew 17:24-27)

REALITY 6
You must make major adjustments in your life to join God in what He is doing.

"Any of you who does not give up everything he has cannot be my disciple" (Luke 14:33).

- God's revelation is your invitation to adjust your life to Him.

- God desires absolute surrender.

- You adjust to a Person.

- Obedience requires adjustments.

- You cannot stay where you are and go with God.

- Obedience is costly to you and those around you.

REALITY 6
(continued)

- You can trust God with your family.

- Obedience requires total dependence on God to work through you.

- "It" never works. God works.

EXAMPLES	NON-EXAMPLES
Noah and the ark	The rich young ruler
Abram leaving Ur/Haran	
Moses to Egypt	
David to be king	
Amos to preach	
Jonah	
Peter, Andrew, James, John	
Matthew	
Saul	

REALITY 6
(continued)

Kinds of Adjustments

Circumstances

job, home, finances

Relationships

family, friends, business associates

Thinking

prejudices, methods, your potential

Commitments

family, church, job, plans, tradition

Actions

prayer, giving, serving

Beliefs

God, His purposes, His ways, your relationship to Him

REALITY 7
You come to know God by experience as you obey Him and He accomplishes His work through you.

" 'If you love me, you will obey what I command. Whoever has my commands and obeys them, he is the one who loves me. He who loves me will be loved by my Father, and I too will love him and show myself to him. If anyone loves me, he will obey my teaching. My Father will love him, and we will come to him and make our home with him. He who does not love me will not obey my teaching' " (John 14:15,21,23-24).

REALITY 7
(continued)

1. Obey what you already know to be God's will. Obey His commands.

2. Affirmation comes after obedience.

3. Obedience is the outward expression of your love of God.

4. Disobedience is costly. God does not always give second chances.

5. If you have an obedience problem, you have a love problem.

6. If you love God, you will obey Him.

7. The reward for obedience and love is that God will reveal Himself to you.

REALITY 7
(continued)

8. God reveals Himself to His people by what He does.

- Israel at the Red Sea (Exodus 14:13,18,25,31)

- Rahab's testimony (Joshua 2:9-11)

- Stone markers, Israel's crossing of the Jordan (Joshua 4:24)

- God defeats army attacking Jehoshaphat (2 Chronicles 20:29)

- God enables Daniel to interpret Nebuchadnezzar's dream (Daniel 2:47)

- God delivers Shadrach, Meshach, and Abednego (Daniel 3:28-29)

- The day of Pentecost (Acts 2:11)

- Five thousand believers (Acts 4:4)

- Dorcas raised from the dead (Acts 9:42)

EXPERIENCING GOD
Knowing and Doing the Will of God

1. God is always at work around you.

2. God pursues a continuing love relationship with you that is real and personal.

3. God invites you to become involved with Him in His work.

4. God speaks by the Holy Spirit through the Bible, prayer, circumstances, and the church to reveal Himself, His purposes, and His ways.

5. God's invitation for you to work with Him always leads you to a crisis of belief that requires faith and action.

6. You must make major adjustments in your life to join God in what He is doing.

7. You come to know God by experience as you obey Him and He accomplishes His work through you.

EXPERIENCING GOD
Knowing and Doing the Will of God

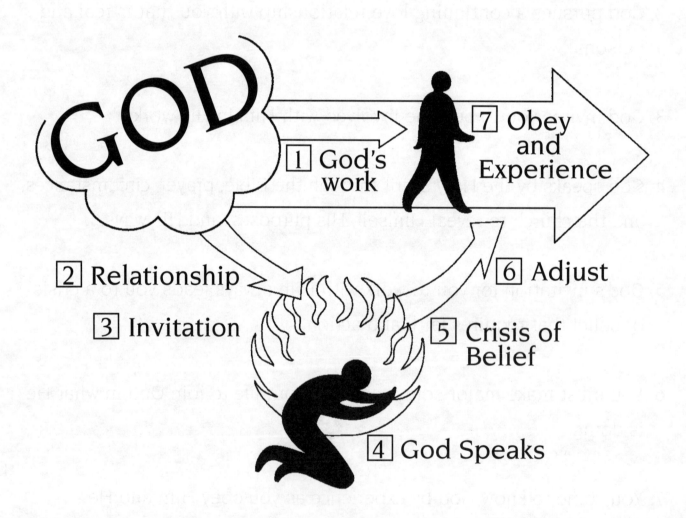

Adult Participant Guide

Welcome to the Experiencing God Weekend! This is your guide through the adult teaching sessions. Take notes and fill in the blanks as your visiting resource teacher leads you through the seven realities of experiencing God.

* *

TEACHING SESSION 1

Introduction

1. The _____ is your guide for _____ and _____.

2. _____ is your way.

3. To be a _____ of God you must be _____ and remain in the _____ of the _____.

4. To _____ God, you must _____ Him.

5. God is _____. His _____ is always best.

6. God is _____. His _____ are always right.

7. God is _____. He can _____ you to do His will.

Reality 1

God is _____ at _____ around you.

Jesus' Example

- The _____ has been _____ right up to now.
- Now _____ has Me _____.
- I do _____ on My own _____.
- I do what I see the _____ already is doing.
- The _____ loves _____.
- He shows me _____ that He, Himself, is _____.

Notes

_____

_____

_____

_____

How do we follow and serve God?

1. Find out _____ the Master is, then that is _____ you need to be.

2. _____ to see where God is _____ and _____ Him.

3. The right questions is: _____ _____ _____ _____?

TEACHING SESSION 2

Reality 2

God _____ a continuing _____ relationship with you that is _____ and _____.

Can you describe your relationship with God by sincerely saying, "I love you with all my heart"?

- Everything in your _____ life, everything about _____ Him and _____ Him, everything about _____ His will, depends on the _____ of your love relationship.

- A _____ relationship with _____ is more important than any other single _____ in your life.

- God created you for a _____ relationship that is _____ and _____.

- The constant _____ of God is the most _____ part of your life and ministry.

- God _____ you not for _____ but for _____.

- Let your present be _____ and _____ by what you are to become in _____, not by your _____.

- Your _____ is more important to God than what you do. God develops _____ to match the _____.

Notes

_____

_____

_____

_____

_____

APG-4

A LOVE RELATIONSHIP

Read the following Scripture passages that speak of a love relationship. As you read, emphasize the word *love* (or any form of it, such as *loves*) by circling it each time it appears.

"This day I call heaven and earth as witnesses against you that I have set before you life and death, blessings and curses. Now choose life, so that you and your children may live and that you may love the Lord your God, listen to his voice, and hold fast to him. For the Lord is your life" (Deuteronomy 30:19-20).

" 'For God so loved the world that he gave his one and only son, that whoever believes in him shall not perish but have eternal life' " (John 3:16).

" 'Whoever has my commands and obeys them, he is the one who loves me. He who loves me will be loved by my Father, and I too will love him and show myself to him' " (John 14:21).

"Who shall separate us from the love of Christ? Shall trouble or hardship or persecution or famine or nakedness or danger or sword? No, in all these things we are more than conquerors through him who loved us. Neither height nor depth, nor anything else in all creation, will be able to separate us from the love of God that is in Christ Jesus our Lord" (Romans 8:35,37,39).

"This is how we know what love is: Jesus Christ laid down his life for us. And we ought to lay down our lives for our brothers" (1 John 3:16).

"This is how God showed his love among us: He sent his one and only Son into the world that we might live through him. This is love: not that we loved God, but that he loved us and sent his Son as an atoning sacrifice for our sins. We love because he first loved us" (1 John 4:9-10,19).

Using the preceding Scripture passages, answer the following questions.

1. Who is your "life"? _____

2. In what ways has God demonstrated His love for us? _____
_____

3. How can we show our love for God? _____
_____

4. What does God promise to do in response to our loving Him? _____
_____

5. Who loved first, you or God? _____

Reality 3

God _____ you to become _____ with Him in His _____.

- You never find God _____ persons to dream up what they _____ to do for Him. He takes the _____.

- _____ what God is about to do where you are is more _____ than _____ God what you want to do for Him.

- God's _____ of His activity is an _____ for you to join Him.

- You cannot know the _____ of God unless He takes the _____ to reveal it to you.

- There are some things that only _____ can do. When you see one of these things _____, you can know _____ is at work.

Notes

_____

_____

_____

_____

_____

Things Only God Can Do

- God _____ people to Himself.

- God _____ people to seek after Him.

- God _____ spiritual truth.

- God _____ the world of guilt regarding sin.

- God _____ the world of righteousness.

- God _____ the world of judgment.

When you want to know what God is doing around you:

1. _____ and _____ to see what God does next.

2. Make the _____ between your _____ and what happens next.

3. Find out what _____ is already _____.

4. Ask _____ questions …
   - How can I _____ for you?
   - What can I _____ for you?
   - Do you want to _____?
   - What do you see as the greatest _____ in your life?
   - What is the most significant _____ happening in your life right now?
   - Would you tell me what _____ is doing in your life?
   - What is God _____ to the surface in your life?
   - What particular _____ has God given you?

5. _____.

6. Be ready to make the necessary _____ in order to join _____ in what He is doing.

TEACHING SESSION 3

Reality 4

God speaks by the Holy Spirit through the _____, _____, circumstances, and the _____ to reveal Himself, His _____, and His _____.

"He who belongs to God hears what God says. The reason you do not hear is that you do not belong to God" (John 8:47).

1. In the Old Testament _____ spoke in many ways. _____ God spoke is the _____ important factor, not _____ He spoke.

   a. When God spoke, it was usually _____ to that individual.
   b. When God spoke, the person was _____ God was speaking.
   c. When God spoke, the person _____ what God said.
   d. When God spoke, that was the _____ with God.

2. In the Gospels God spoke by His _____ (see Hebrews 1:1-2).

3. In Acts and to the present God speaks by the _____ _____ (see John 14:26; 16:13-14).

4. Knowing God's _____ comes from an intimate _____ relationship with Him.

5. God speaks when He has a _____ in mind for your life.

6. The moment God speaks to you is God's _____.

7. You never _____ truth. Truth is _____ (see John 8:47).

8. God reveals Himself to _____ your faith.

9. God reveals His purposes so you _____ do His work.

10. God reveals His ways so you can _____ His purposes.

Notes

_____
_____
_____
_____
_____
_____

Reality 5

God's _____ for you to work with Him always leads you to a _____ of _____ that requires _____ and _____.

1. What is faith? _____
   _____

2. What is an opposite of faith? _____
   _____

3. How important is it for your faith to be in God and what He says rather than what you or someone else decides would be a nice thing to have happen?
   _____
   _____

- The crisis of belief is a _____ point where you must make a decision. You must _____ what you really _____ about God.

- An _____ with God requires faith and action.

- Encounters with God are _____.

- Our world is not _____ God because we are not _____ anything that only God can do.

- What you do in response to God's _____ (invitation) reveals what you _____ about God.

- Faith is in a _____.

- True faith requires _____.

Notes

TEACHING SESSION 4

Reality 6

You must make major _____ in your life to _____ God in what He is doing.

"Any of you who does not give up everything he has cannot be my disciple" (Luke 14:33).

- God's _____ is your _____ to adjust your life to Him.

- God desires absolute _____.

- You _____ to a Person.

- _____ requires adjustments.

APG-10

_____

- You cannot _____ where you are and _____ with God.

- _____ is costly to you and those around you.

- You can _____ God with your family.

- _____ requires total _____ on God to work through you.

- "_____" never works. _____ works.

EXAMPLES	NON-EXAMPLES
_____	_____
_____	_____
_____	_____
_____	_____
_____	_____
_____	_____
_____	_____
_____	_____
_____	_____

Notes

_____

_____

_____

_____

Kinds of Adjustments

In your _____ (job, home, finances, etc.)

In your _____ (family, friends, business associates, etc.)

In your _____ (prejudices, methods, your potential, etc.)

In your _____ (family, church, job, plans, tradition, etc.)

In your _____ (prayer, giving, serving, etc.)

In your _____ (God, His purposes, His ways, your relationship to Him, etc.)

Reality 7

You come to know God by _____ as you _____ Him and He _____ His work through you.

" "If you love me, you will obey what I command. Whoever has my commands and obeys them, he is the one who loves me. He who loves me will be loved by my Father, and I too will love him and show myself to him. If anyone loves me, he will obey my teaching. My Father will love him, and we will come to him and make our home with him. He who does not love me will not obey my teaching' " (John 14:15,21,23-24).

1. _____ what you already know to be God's _____. Obey His _____.

2. _____ comes after _____.

3. Obedience is the _____ expression of your _____ of God.

4. _____ is costly. God does not always give _____ chances.

5. If you have an _____ problem, you have a _____ problem.

6. If you _____ God, you will _____ Him.

7. The _____ for obedience and love is that God will _____ Himself to you.

8. God _____ Himself to His people by _____ He does.

Notes

SPIRITUAL MARKERS WORKSHEET
(*For use in final Small-group Discussion.*)

Name: _____ **Date:** _____

Identifying My Spiritual Markers
Think about your life and ask God to guide you to identify your spiritual markers. These may be from your family heritage, salvation experience, significant decisions, and so forth. What are some of the times of transition, decision, or direction in your life when you clearly knew God guided you? Write these down in the order they happened. Use extra paper if needed.

1. _____
2. _____
3. _____
4. _____
5. _____
6. _____
7. _____
8. _____
9. _____
10. _____

What God Is Showing Me
Ask the Lord to reveal what the pattern of these markers mean for you. Write down your impressions.

_____

_____

Adjustments God Wants Me to Make
Ask the Lord to reveal any adjustment He wants you to make in your life so you can join Him where He is working and for Him to accomplish His work through you.

_____

_____

Youth Section

Weekend Schedule for Youth

Thursday
5:00 p.m. — Churchwide 24-hour prayer vigil

Friday
6:00 p.m. — Churchwide fellowship meal
6:45 p.m. — General session for everyone
Music and testimonies
7:30 p.m. — *Lift High the Torch*, Youth Session 1
9:15 p.m. — Reconvene for closing praise time
Pair hosts and guests

Saturday
9:00 a.m. — *Lift High the Torch*, Youth Session 2
11:30 a.m. — Testimonies and prayer time with everyone
12:15 p.m. — Lunch
(Option: The church might choose to omit lunch and the afternoon activities can take place from 11:30 a.m. to 12:30 p.m. Everyone is dismissed at 12:30 for the afternoon.)
1:00 p.m. — *Lift High the Torch*, Youth Session 3
2:00 p.m. — Dismiss for the afternoon
6:00 p.m. — Churchwide fellowship meal
6:45 p.m. — General session for everyone
Music and testimonies
7:30 p.m. — *Lift High the Torch*, Youth Session 4
9:30 p.m. — Adjourn for the day

Sunday
9:30 a.m. — Sunday School (adults and youth meet together)
10:45 a.m. — Worship service
Testimonies and commitment time
6:00 p.m. — Evaluation time: What is God saying to you?
Commitment to *Experiencing God: Knowing and Doing the Will of God, Youth Edition*

Elements of the Weekend

Prayer Vigil
Youth are an important part of the 24-hour prayer vigil that begins Thursday at 5:00 p.m. before the Experiencing God Weekend. Of the four people praying each hour, one should be a youth. Or the youth might accept the late night hours on Thursday or the early morning hours on Friday as their time during the prayer vigil.

Lift High the Torch
The material for the youth teaching sessions during the weekend is *Lift High the Torch-An Invitation to Experiencing God* by Henry Blackaby. This study asks the question, How can youth live holy lives in a world filled with sin? The visiting youth resource teacher will lead youth to discover that holiness means living life in a way that serves and pleases God. A growing relationship with God serves like a torch lighting the way to guide others to Him. Living a life of holiness ensures God's best for youth. And God has provided everything youth need to live this holy life. What a great way to introduce youth to a study of *Experiencing God: Knowing and Doing the Will of God!*

The following information illustrates how to include *Lift High the Torch* in the weekend schedule. A copy of the book should be provided for each participant. They will use the book during the sessions and will want to complete it at home later.

Numbered activities are the titles of the suggestions in "During the Session" in the Group Learning Activities in the back of Lift High the Torch. Recommended time frames have been adjusted to allow opportunity for more group participation. Bulleted activities have been added for the Experiencing God Weekend. Adapt any of these ideas to meet your needs and those of the church.

Friday (7:30–9:15 p.m.)
Youth Session 1: Where God Is Working
1. Take Off Your Shoes (God Gets Our Attention) (10 minutes)
- Introductions: Name, grade, job or hobby, one interesting fact. (10 minutes)
- Welcome visiting youth and express appreciation for their leadership. (5 minutes)
2. Seven Realities (5 minutes)
- Testimony of visiting youth. (10 minutes)
3. Holy-ness? (It's More Than Needing to Get Your Shoes Fixed) (10 minutes)
4. Holy Rebels (Then) (20 minutes)
5. Holy Rebels (Now) (20 minutes)
6. Put On Holiness (Letting God Prepare You) (15 minutes)

Saturday (9:00–11:30 a.m.)
Youth Session 2: Who Goes with God?
1. Winning the Game (20 minutes)
2. Pressing On… (20 minutes)
- Testimony of visiting youth. (10 minutes)
- Break (30 minutes)
3. Pressing On Toward What? (15 minutes)
4. Pressing How? (15 minutes)
- Testimony of visiting youth. (20 minutes)
5. Pressing On with Whom? (20 minutes)

Saturday (1:00–2:00 p.m.)
Youth Session 3: Following God
1. The High Cost of Holiness (10 minutes)
2. The Rewards (10 minutes)
3. The Struggle for Holiness (20 minutes)
- Testimony of visiting youth. (5 minutes)
4. Choosing to Be Holy (5 minutes)
5. Aiming for Holiness (10 minutes)

Saturday (7:30–9:30 p.m.)
Youth Session 4: Joining God
1. Patterns of Growth Toward Holiness (15 minutes)
2. Choices of Holiness (20 minutes)
- Testimony of visiting youth. (10 minutes)
3. Experiencing God Course Overview (20 minutes)
- Testimony of visiting youth. (15 minutes)
4. Life Commitments (15 minutes)
5. Decision Time (10 minutes)
- Instructions about Sunday morning and evening activities. (5 minutes)
- Appreciation to visiting youth for their leadership. (5 minutes)
6. Closing Prayer (5 minutes)

Sunday School
The time in Sunday School builds a bridge between those who attended the weekend and those who did not. Adults and youth meet together for Sunday School as a large group. Limit record taking to a head count and collection of offering envelopes. The weekend coordinator or general chairperson opens the Sunday School time, welcomes people, makes announcements, takes up offering envelopes, and turns the meeting over to the adult resource teacher. The adult resource teacher gives an overview of the study being introduced. He may use adult and youth visiting team members to give testimonies. The adult resource teacher dismisses Sunday School.

Morning Worship
There are two main objectives in the worship service: 1) the adult resource teacher speaks on the theme of the study being introduced that weekend, and 2) people will be given the opportunity during the invitation to make a commitment to Christ. If testimonies are included in the service, visiting youth team members or church youth should be included.

Sunday Evening Praise and Evaluation Service
The Sunday evening praise and evaluation service is the only activity scheduled on Sunday evening. Youth activities should be canceled for this one

Sunday. The service starts whenever the usual Sunday evening activities begin, and lasts for an hour and a half or longer. The service begins with praise choruses, prayer, and welcome of guests by the pastor, along with an explanation that the service will not be the usual Sunday evening service. After necessary announcements, the general chairperson gives a personal testimony of what God did in his or her life during the weekend. Church members are asked to share what the Lord taught them during the weekend. Youth should be encouraged to participate. This can be a worshipful time for the congregation. Evaluation forms used during the service offer youth an opportunity to evaluate the weekend and sign up for *Experiencing God: Knowing and Doing the Will of God, Youth Edition*. The general chairperson will explain how the study will be offered: the number of small groups expected, when and where they will meet, and who will be facilitating each age group.

VISITING YOUTH LEADERS

Guidelines for Youth Resource Teachers
- Complete *Experiencing God: Knowing and Doing the Will of God, Youth Edition* (ISBN 0-8054-9925-3) and *Lift High the Torch—An Invitation to Experiencing God, Youth* (ISBN 0-8054-9847-8).
- Remember that you are introducing the study. Don't teach the total content. Introduce the seven realities and make personal application.
- Make the study personal. Get it in your heart before you attempt to teach it.
- Stay with the time frame for each teaching session.
- Work closely with the weekend coordinator before and during the weekend.
- Work with visiting youth and schedule each one to give a personal testimony sometime during the weekend.
- Know the direction each session is taking. Be familiar with the material.
- Continually evaluate the weekend. Ask for comments from youth, the pastor, church staff, church members, and visiting youth team members.
- Keep the study simple and understandable.

Guidelines for Visiting Youth
- Complete *Experiencing God: Knowing and Doing the Will of God, Youth Edition* (ISBN 0-8054-9925-3) and *Lift High the Torch—An Invitation to Experiencing God, Youth* (ISBN 0-8054-9847-8).
- Be prepared to share a testimony about the value of studying *Experiencing God: Knowing and Doing the Will of God, Youth Edition*.
- Be available to talk individually with church youth about your spiritually journey and experiences.
- Enthusiastically participate in all youth sessions. Don't dominate discussions but add to them as appropriate.
- Be grateful for the opportunity to minister with church youth during the weekend.

Children's Section

Weekend Schedule for Children

Friday
6:00 p.m. — Churchwide fellowship meal
6:45 p.m. — General session for everyone
Music and testimonies
7:30 p.m. — Children's Session 1
9:15 p.m. — Reconvene for closing praise time
Pair hosts and guests

Saturday
9:00 a.m. — Children's Session 2
10:15 a.m. — Break, snacks, and outside activities (weather permitting)
10:45 a.m. — Children's Session 2 continued
11:30 a.m. — Testimonies and prayer time with everyone
12:15 p.m. — Lunch
(Option: The church might choose to omit lunch and the afternoon activities can take place from 11:30 a.m. to 12:30 p.m. Everyone is dismissed at 12:30 for the afternoon.)
1:00 p.m. — Children's Session 3
2:00 p.m. — Dismiss for the afternoon
6:00 p.m. — Churchwide fellowship meal
6:45 p.m. — General session for everyone
Music and testimonies
7:30 p.m. — Children's Session 4
9:30 p.m. — Adjourn for the day

Sunday
9:30 a.m. — Sunday School (adults and youth meet together)
10:45 a.m. — Worship service
Testimonies and commitment time
6:00 p.m. — Evaluation time: What is God saying to you?
Commitment to the study

Resource Teacher Plans
(*Adjust according to the church's needs.*)

Children participating in the weekend will be learning in their groups the same principles of *Experiencing God: Knowing and Doing the Will of God* that adults and youth are learning in their groups. The children will study four of the seven realities.

Depending on the size of the church and the number of children attending the weekend, there may be more than one visiting children's resource teacher. If so, group children so there are a similar number in each group. If more than one group is needed, group by younger and older children.

You should have completed *Experiencing God: Knowing and Doing the Will of God*. These principles should flow out of your life to the children.

Seven Realities of Experiencing God
(simplified for children)
1. *God is always working.*
2. *God loves you.*
3. *God wants you to work with Him.*
4. *God speaks to you.*
5. *God wants you to trust Him.*
6. *God wants you to change to please Him.*
7. *God allows you to know Him better when you obey Him.*

The goal of the weekend is to help children understand that they can experience God by knowing His will. Make a copy of the Children's Workbook beginning on page 69 for each child. If some of the activities are too difficult for younger children, pair them with an older child or adult. The teaching

material in the following section will help you plan your group time with the children. Specific directions for teachers are in parentheses.

Friday Evening (7:30-9:15)
Children's Session 1
(Children are in the worship center with adults until 7:30 p.m. When you are dismissed from the worship center, go to the children's room. Get acquainted with the children as they enter.)

Reality 1: *God is always working.*
Have you ever wondered what it would be like to have lived in Bible times? To see how God worked in the lives of His people? God is still working in the lives of His people today. Even as boys and girls you can begin doing some things that will better help you understand God's will for you. Tonight we will look at Bible stories about how God worked in the lives of His people.

Memory Verse
" 'My Father is always at His work to this very day, and I, too, am working' " (John 5:17). (Repeat the verse three times as a group. Then ask several children to repeat it individually.)

Listening Questions
(Print these on poster board to help the children remember what to listen for. This is especially true for younger children.)

As you listen to the Bible story, listen to find the answers to these questions.
1. What message did God have Elijah tell King Ahab?
2. What bird fed Elijah while he was hiding from King Ahab?
3. How did God care for Elijah in Zarephath?
4. How was the widow rewarded for her kindness to Elijah?
5. Why did it take courage for Elijah to challenge the priests of Baal?
6. How did Elijah show courage when he prayed for rain?

(Explain to the children that they need to listen carefully as you tell the story so they can be ready to answer the questions.)

Bible Story (1 Kings 17:7-24; 18:16-45)
Can anyone tell us what a prophet is? The story tonight is about Elijah (*ih LIGH juh*) who was one of God's prophets. Many times people did not like prophets because they told other people how God wanted them to live. There were many people who loved God and worshiped Him. King Ahab (AY *hab*) was a king in Israel and He did not love God as the other kings had. He was not a good ruler and God was not happy with the things King Ahab did.

One day Elijah the prophet, who loved God very much, came to King Ahab and said, "The Lord is not happy with you." Ahab couldn't care less about what God thought and did not plan for that to make any difference in the things he was doing that displeased God. Elijah told him that because of this there would not be any rain or dew for the next few years unless Elijah said so.

God wanted to take care of Elijah and told him to leave that city and go to a place by a small river and hide there. While Elijah was there he had clear, cold water to drink. God sent ravens every morning and evening to bring food for Elijah to eat.

Elijah stayed there until the river went dry. Why did the river go dry? God told Elijah to go to a city called Zarephath (ZAR *ih fath*) and there he would find a woman who would take care of him. Elijah obeyed God and went into the city. He was wondering where he would find this special woman. When he got to the city, Elijah saw a woman who was gathering sticks for a fire. He was very thirsty and asked if she could give him a drink of water. She agreed and as she left to get the water, Elijah asked her for some bread to go with the water. The lady told Elijah that she would love to help him but she did not have any bread in her house. She said, "I only have a handful of flour and some oil in a jar. I plan to use these sticks and cook a meal for my son and me. It will be our last meal. When this is gone, then we'll die." Elijah told her to go on as she planned, but first make a small loaf of bread for him. He told her God would provide for her. He said the Lord had told him there would be enough oil and enough flour for her until God sent rain on the land again. The woman obeyed Elijah, went to her house and made a small loaf of bread for Elijah and poured him some cool water. This used all her flour and oil. Elijah told her to make some bread for herself and her son. She looked at him rather puzzled because she had used the last flour and oil for Elijah. But when she reached in the flour jar there was more flour. And in the olive oil jug there was more oil. She was so happy! God had provided for her just a Elijah had said.

About three years passed and Elijah stood before King Ahab. During these years there had been no rain. Elijah told King Ahab that he and his family had not worshiped God, but worshiped false gods and idols. Elijah looked at the people who had once worshiped Yahweh (YAH *weh*) the Lord and were now bowing down to Baal (BAY *uhl*). He had all the people come to Mt. Carmel (KAHR *m'l*) and bring two bulls to be offered as sacrifices. He wanted the priests of Baal to kill one and place it on their altar. He told them not to light a fire to burn the sacrifice. He would kill the other bull and place it on the altar of the Lord God of Israel. He told the people that whoever sends the fire to burn the sacrifice, let Israel worship Him. The people agreed and the priests of Baal killed their bull and placed it on the altar.

They danced and called out to Baal to send fire to burn their sacrifice. This went on for a long time and still no fire came down. Elijah even made fun of them and said, "Surely he is a god! Perhaps he is in deep thought, or busy, or traveling. Maybe he is sleeping and needs to be awakened. Shout louder!" The priests did. Still nothing happened.

Then Elijah built his altar and dug a large ditch around it. He ordered the men to come and fill four large water jars and pour the water over the sacrifice. He had the men do this three times and the water ran down and filled the ditch.

Elijah knelt in front of the altar and prayed to God. There was a large crackling sound and fire fell from God in heaven. It burned not only the sacrifice, but the wood and the altar. It even dried up the water in the ditch!

The people bowed down and said, "The Lord is God." Elijah told King Ahab that he could go eat and drink because it was going to rain. The king looked around and he saw only a clear, blue sky. How was it going to rain? Elijah knelt and prayed and sent his servant to check the sky. Still no sign of rain. He did this seven times. The people were beginning to think that Baal was the lord of rain and storms and maybe Yahweh could send fire, but not rain. On the seventh time the servant came back and said he saw a small cloud about the size of a man's hand. Elijah told the servant to tell King Ahab to go home before the rains fell hard.

In a short time the sky was dark and there were large billowy clouds. The wind began to blow and soon a few drops of rain started to fall. Then there was heavy rain. I would imagine that Elijah shouted, "Praise the Lord!" as he ran all the way back to the town of Jezreel (JEZ *reel*).

(Go over the listening questions that were given before the story. Ask the children to tell some ways that they saw God at work in the life of Elijah and also in the woman who helped him.)

George Mueller
(Share with the children about George Mueller and his walk of faith.)

George Mueller was a pastor in England during the 19th century. He noticed that God's people had become discouraged. They no longer looked to God to do anything unusual. They no longer trusted God to answer prayers.

God led George to pray. George's prayers were for God to lead him to do something the people would see as an act of God. George wanted them to learn that God was a faithful, prayer-answering God. He came upon the verse Psalm 81:10, "Open wide your mouth and I will fill it." God began to lead him in a walk of faith that became an outstanding testimony to all who heard his story.

When George felt led of God to do some work, he prayed for the resources needed and told no one the need. He wanted everyone to know that God had provided for the need because of an answer to prayer and faith.

During his ministry in Bristol, England, George started the Scriptural Knowledge Institute for the distribution of Scripture and for religious education. He also began an orphanage for children whose parents could not take care of them. By the time of his death, God used George Mueller to build four orphanages that cared for 2,000 children at that time. Over 10,000 children were provided for through the orphanages. He distributed over 8 million dollars that had been given to him in answer to prayer. Many times during the days at the orphanage, there would not be enough food for meals. They would gather around the table and pray. When they finished there would be someone at the door with bread, milk, or some food item. When he died at 93, his worldly possessions were valued at $800.

(Ask if anyone would like to share some ways God has worked in their life or the life of someone they know. Be prepared to share your experiences if the children are hesitant. Help the children understand that right now God is working all around them and in their lives. They need to know that the Holy Spirit and the Word of God will instruct them and help them know when and where God is working.)

Activities
Provide the following activities during the remainder of the session.
- Worksheet 1
- Worksheet 2
- Worksheet 3 (younger children)
- Worksheet 4 (older children)
- If time allows, show a *Secret Adventures* video tape.
  Secret Adventures Video Series (optional)

  Spin   (ISBN 0-8054-8361-6)

  Snap   (ISBN 0-8054-8362-4)

  Smash (ISBN 0-8054-8363-2)

  Shrug (ISBN 0-8054-8365-9)

  Snag   (ISBN 0-8054-8364-0)

  Slam   (ISBN 0-8054-8366-7)

  Split (ISBN 0-8054-8367-5)

Saturday Morning (9:00-11:30 a.m.)
Children's Session 2
(Children go directly to their rooms when they arrive. They can finish any activities they did not complete Friday night until the other children arrive. The morning schedule should include:
9:00 a.m.–Bible story/activity time
10:15 a.m.–Break, snack, and outside activities (weather permitting)
10:45 a.m.–Bible story/activity time

Reality 2: *God loves you.*
There are many people who love you. This morning we are going to see how God loves us and wants us to love Him.

Memory Verses
"Jesus replied, 'Love the Lord your God with all your heart and with all your soul and with all your mind' " (Matthew 22:37).

" 'For God so loved the world that He gave His only begotten Son, that whosoever believeth in Him should not perish but have everlasting life' " (John 3:16, KJV).

(Repeat the verses three times as a group. Then ask several children to repeat them individually.)

Bible Stories
God loves us and wants us to love Him. God created us for this purpose. We ought to be able to love God with all our hearts. He wants all of us, not just the parts that we want to give Him.

When we have problems with each other, we don't have the kind of love relationship with God that we need. Because God loves us, He knows what is best for us.

Think about a time when you really wanted something and you didn't get it. What did you think at the time? Did you think that Mother and Daddy were just being mean, or that because they loved you, they knew what would be best for you and did not want you to have something that would bring harm to you in some way?

God loves us more than our parents. God wants us to love Him and live our lives to please Him. Even now we should begin letting God mold and shape our lives the way He wants to.

There are some things that will help us to have a loving relationship with God. The most important would be to have a quiet time with God. We are never too young to begin spending time alone with God. Ask Mother and Daddy to help you find 15 minutes during the day or evening when you can read your Bible and pray. Then share with them what you have learned.

Another way that we can deepen our love relationship with God is through worship. There are many ways that we worship God. We can worship God by attending church, singing songs of praise, giving our money, and praying. We can read books about men and women in the Bible who loved God and walked with Him as well as men and women today. Look for things in their lives that they did because they loved God. Could you do some of the same things?

Let's look at one or two Bible stories that tell of people who walked with God in a love relationship.

Genesis 2: (Read this chapter to the children out of the Bible or tell the story in your own words.) God created Adam to have fellowship with Him. *Fellowship* means that we have a loving relationship with God. After God created everything and made Adam, He realized that there was not anyone to be a help to Adam. God gave Adam Eve to be his wife and love him. They enjoyed the beauty of God's creation together and they walked and talked with God each day.

Genesis 6-9: (Study this passage of Scripture and be able to tell the story to the children in your own words.) Noah was a man who loved God. Noah and his family were different—the other people did not love God. Noah built an altar and worshiped God there. Because of the love relationship between God and Noah, God established a covenant with Noah and his descendants.

Each time God took the initiative for each person in the Old Testament to experience Him in a personal fellowship of love. That means God always took the first step toward people so they could know Him and have a loving relationship with Him.

This is true in the New Testament as well. Jesus came to the disciples and chose them to be with Him and experience His love. He came to Paul on the Damascus Road. (Share briefly the story of Paul on the Damascus Road as recorded in Acts 9:1-19.)

Remember, God always takes the initiative in loving us.

(Use one or more of the following Bible stories after the morning break to reinforce Reality 2. Tell the Bible story in your words if possible. Adam and Eve (Genesis 3:20-21); Hagar (Genesis 16:1-13); Solomon (1 Kings 3:5-13; 4:29-30); the twelve disciples (Mark 6:7-13); John (Acts 12:1-17; Revelation 1:9-20). In studying these verses and sharing the stories with the children, find one fact in each account that lets you know they had a personal, real relationship with God.)

Activities
Provide the following activities during the remainder of the morning session.
* Break, snacks, and outside activities (weather permitting)
* People God Loved Bible Search (older children)
* Noah's Ark Hunt (younger children)
* Worksheet 5
* Worksheet 6

People God Loved Bible Search
(Before the children arrive, print the following Scripture references on separate construction paper hearts:

Saul/Paul	Acts 9:1-8; 17-19
Noah	Genesis 6:8-21
Children	Mark 10:13-16
Zachaeus	Luke 19:1-10
Ten lepers	Luke 17:11-19
Blind Bartimaeus	Mark 10:46-52
Adam and Eve	Genesis 2
Woman at well	John 4:4-15

PERSON	SCRIPTURE	HOW LOVED

On a poster board or large sheet of paper, make a chart with three columns titled *Person, Scripture,* and *How Loved* (see illustration at the top of page 9).

Place the heart-shaped cards around the room where the children in the group can easily find them. Place the poster on a table or wall near where your group will be working. Have Bibles, construction paper, scissors, and markers available.

As the children arrive in the group, have them search the room to find the heart-shaped Scripture references. Have each pupil look up and read at least one reference. When the children finish reading their passages, ask them to tell briefly how God showed His love to each person described. Discuss how each one discovered and fulfilled God's plan for his or her life.

Have the pupils cut out heart shapes or rectangular shapes on which to write a brief description of how God showed His love. Place shapes with answers in appropriate places on the chart.

Noah's Ark Hunt
(This game will be played like Concentration™ or Memory™. Use 16 or 18 cards. Write the names of animals or use animal stickers. You will need two of the same animal for two of each of the cards. The children take turns turning up the cards until they find a match.)

Saturday Afternoon (1:00-2:00 p.m.)
Children's Session 3
(Spend the first half of this one-hour session working on the three memory verses the children are learning. Review the verses several times.)

(Show one of the *Secret Adventures* videos and discuss the biblical teachings reflected in the video.

(Encourage the children to come back for the Saturday evening session.)

Saturday Evening (7:30-9:30 p.m.)
Children's Session 4
(Children are with adults until 7:30 p.m. and then move to their area for the remainder of the evening. At the beginning of the session, work on activities not completed earlier.)

Memory Verses
(Repeat the verses the children have memorized as a group. Then ask several children to repeat them individually.)

Reality 5: *God wants you to trust Him.*
What does it mean to trust someone. (Allow several children to respond.) Tonight you are going to learn that God wants you to trust Him.

Bible Stories
Daniel 3: There are many stories in the Bible that help us understand what a crisis of belief means. A crisis of belief happens when God tells us to do something, but we aren't sure how to do it or if we can do it. We're not sure what to do or think. When we trust God, we will do what He tells us to do even if we aren't sure how it will be done.

Daniel 3 contains an example of this and how God took care of three young men who trusted God and were obedient—Shadrach (SHAD *rak*), Meshach (MEE *shak*), and Abednego (*uh* BED-*nih goh*).

When the music sounded, all the people rushed out of their houses and fell on their knees to worship the image of the king. It was a tall idol–maybe 95 feet high and 9 feet wide. (Compare this with the size of something familiar to the children.) The king had ordered all the people to bow down and worship him every time the music sounded. If they didn't do this, they would be thrown into a fiery furnace. The people were afraid not to obey the king.

One day a messenger came to the king and said that there were three young men who refused to bow down and worship him. This upset the king and he demanded that the three men be brought to him. They were Shadrach, Meshack, and Abednego. When they came before the king, he asked, "Is it true that you won't bow down to my image?" "Yes," they replied. "You see, our God lives in heaven and He is the one we worship. We will worship only the true God."

This made the king very angry. How could anyone dare to disobey him? He told his men to heat the furnace hotter than it had ever been before and then throw the men into it. He would teach the people what would happen if they disobeyed his orders!

Shadrach, Meshach, and Abednego were tied up and thrown into the hot furnace. The furnace was so hot that the men who threw them in the furnace died from the high heat.

The king looked into the furnace. He was sure that he would see the bodies of the three young men. But guess what? He saw not only the three young men walking around, but there was a fourth person in the furnace with them. Do you know who that fourth person was? The king said he looked like the son of God.

The king was so surprised he called to Shadrach, Meshach, and Abednego and told them to come out of the fire. They stepped out of the furnace and the king was amazed. They didn't smell like smoke; their hair was not singed; and their clothes weren't burned!

The king turned in astonishment and spoke to the people. He said, "The God of these men is a powerful God. He sent His angel to protect them while they were in the furnace. Never say anything against their God. Only He can perform this kind of miracle."

What was the crisis of belief that Shadrach, Meshach, and Abednego faced? How did God respond to their obedience to Him?

1 *Samuel* 17:4-14, 38-51: (Tell this story in your own words or use the following account that has been adapted from *Precious Moments, Stories from the Bible*.)

The Israelites (IZ *ray el ights*) were in the middle of a battle with their enemies, the Philistines (*fih* LISS *teens*). Their enemy had a very good soldier named Goliath (*guh* LIGH *uhth*). To make matters worse, he was a giant! He would make fun of the Israelites and tease them. He told them that if they would send someone over to fight him and kill him then the Philistines would be their slaves. But if he killed the Israelite then they would become slaves to the Philistines.

Goliath stood over nine feet tall. He was a monster of a man! Who could the Israelites find that would fight him? Every man who went over to look at him ran back afraid.

One day David, who was the little brother of several of the soldiers, came to bring food to them. He heard the men talking and he heard Goliath teasing them. He said, "I'll fight the giant. I'm not afraid of him. I am on God's side and He will take care of me." He ran off to find three stones to place in his slingshot. The soldiers almost laughed. David was so small. He was so small that the Israelites didn't even have armor to fit him. David was determined to fight the giant.

David walked out across the field to face Goliath. Everything got quiet. When the giant saw David, he laughed and asked, "Why are you sending a boy? Do you not have a man?" David was not afraid. He told the giant that even without a lot of weapons, God was with him. God would help David kill the giant.

David kept walking toward Goliath. At just the right time David took a stone out of his pouch and placed it in his slingshot. He whirled it round and round. Before Goliath knew what was happening the

stone left the slingshot and hit Goliath's head. He fell, crashing to the ground. He was dead. David had put his trust in God. God had helped him.

What was the crisis of belief that David faced? How did God respond to David's obedience?

Activities
Provide the following activities during the remainder of the Saturday evening session.
- Mural on the Story of Daniel
- Scripture Verse Puzzles
- Worksheet 7 (older children)
- Worksheet 8 (older children)

Mural on the Story of Daniel
(Have the children turn in their Bibles to Daniel 6:1-24 and read the story about Daniel and the lion's den. Invite them to draw a mural illustrating the story. Have them share with you what Daniel's crisis of belief was and how God took care of him.)

Scripture Verse Puzzle
(Glue the following Scriptures on poster board. Cut them apart between each line. Mix up all the pieces. Let the children choose a piece. Instruct the ones who choose Scripture verses to look them up and read the passage aloud. Other children are to add the other two pieces to form the verse.)

Psalm 56:11
In God I trust.
I will not be afraid.

2 Timothy 1:7
For God did not give us a spirit of timidity, but a spirit of power, of love and of self-discipline.

1 Corinthians 14:33
For God is not a God of disorder
but of peace.

John 14:1
Do not let not your hearts be troubled.
Trust in God; trust also in me.

Sunday Morning and Evening

Sunday School
(Work with the church's children's workers in planning Sunday School. Material is provided, but some churches may prefer to maintain their regular Sunday School schedule.)

Reality 6: *God wants you to change to please Him.*
We all want to please those we love and who love us. This morning you are going to learn how God wants you to change to please Him.

Memory Verse
" 'Any of you who does not give up everything he has cannot be my disciple' " (Luke 14:33).

Listening Questions
Many times in our lives we have to make changes to do what we know is right and what God wants us to do. Abram had to make a major change in his life. Let's look at the story in Genesis and see what happened in the life of Abram.

As you listen to the Bible story, listen to find the answers to these questions. (You may want to print the listening questions on a piece of poster board, especially for younger children.)
1. Who were the members of Abram's family?
2. What was it like to move in Abram's day?
3. Do you think Abram believed and trusted God? Why?
4. How did Abram worship God?
5. What change do you think Abram had to make in his life?

Bible Story
What if one day God told you to make a move? Maybe you knew where you were going but it would be rather hard since you would have to leave your friends, school, and church. Well, God told Abram (AY *bruhm*) to make a move. God wanted him to gather up his family and everything he owned and move to a country God would show him later. It was almost like starting on a journey without a road map! Abram and his wife Sara did just what God asked.

They began packing everything they owned. They had tents, dishes, furniture, animals, and many other things to get ready for the move. Lot (LAHT), who was Abram's nephew, had to pack up also. They had many animals between the two families.

Today when we move, we usually rent a truck or a moving van takes us. We can make a move in several days. Abram did not have a truck or a moving van. He and his family used wagons, horses, and donkeys. It probably took months to make the move. At night they would stop and make camp.

As the next day would come, Abram would wonder, *Where will God take us? What will the land be like? Will there be neighbors?* Each day they came closer and closer to the land God promised. Each day Abram thought, *Maybe this is the day we will reach the land that will be our new home.*

While they were on their journey Abram and Lot went separate ways. Their servants were having trouble getting along and this was causing problems. Lot and Abram decided that it would be better for everyone if they parted ways. Abram let Lot choose the land that he wanted to live in.

God said to Abram, "See the land with the rolling hills? All the land to the north, south, east, and west? This is the land that I am going to give to you." Abram looked and saw all the land and he thanked God for bringing him to his new home.

(Go over the listening questions that were given before the story.)

Activities
(Provide the following activities during the remainder of Sunday School.)
- Mural on the story of Abram's move
- Worksheet 9 (older children)
- Worksheet 10 (older children)

Mural on the Story of Abram's Move
(Have the children reflect on the story about Abram and his family's move. Invite them to draw a mural illustrating the story. Have them share with you how Abram pleased God.)

Morning Worship
(Children will join adults and youth for morning worship.)

Sunday Evening Praise and Evaluation Service
(The Sunday Evening Praise and Evaluation Service is the only activity scheduled for Sunday evening. The service starts whenever the usual Sunday evening activities begin, and lasts for an hour and a half or longer. The service includes praise songs and testimonies. This can be a meaningful time for children as they hear what God has done in the lives of others during the weekend.)

CHILDREN'S WORKBOOK

Welcome to the Experiencing God Weekend! This is your workbook. At the end of the weekend, you will share what you have done with your parents. We have even included a letter to them explaining what we have done together in the children's area. Do your best as you learn about God.

* *

Parents,

This is a workbook that your child worked through this weekend. Please take time to go over the material with him or her. Let him or her explain what we learned about God. It has been our desire for your child to have the opportunity to learn how to experience God even as children and begin to seek His will for his or her life.

During the weekend the children were encouraged to have a quiet time and to begin keeping a journal even if just a line or two. Your child may or may not talk to you about this, but this is something you could do as a family and it would benefit each member.

It is our prayer that the Experiencing God Weekend and the seven realities will become real in your life and that of your family.

Worksheet 1
God Is Always Working

Go across the line and circle every fourth (4th) letter. Write the circled letters in the spaces below to discover the memory verse.

```
C D E M X W V Y O M P F Q T I A Y I E T X U P H M
R W E N B P R E X T I M N W S Q B U A Z N G L P Y
V W A M B A V C X Y A P E S W Z N A M C S T A P I
H T W B I C A Q S P U V W E R X O P B R P X W K R
S Q W T Z I R O D K L T A P N H I X W I N I X S W
Z A V P W A E O P W R Q V A Y P I A D Y N S A A Q
N Y Z A O A A I P N A N E D Q E Z I P A Q T P U B
O Z X V O P Y A A P O T M Q M V W A S D O P I S R
M U C K S O E I P Z X N Q A S G
```

"__ _____ __ _____ __ ___ ____ __ ____ ____ ___ ___, _, ___, __ _____." John 5:17

Worksheet 2
Word Match

Match the words on the left with a similar word on the right.

prophet	bull
king	oil and flour
food	Ahab
idol	raven
God	Elijah
widow	Baal
sacrifice	Yahweh

Draw a picture of one way you see God working around you. Share your picture with your teacher and talk about it.

CW-4

Worksheet 3
Word Search for Younger Children

Each of the words on the right are found in the puzzle. Find them and circle each one.

```
E L I J A H V S R
P B U L L S X S A
F Z I Q X D E W V
I C F L O U R Z E
R P I V I R A I N
E B A A L X S O N
V W I D O W D U Y
```

ELIJAH   BULLS
DEW   RAVEN
FIRE   FLOUR
BAAL   SON
WIDOW   RAIN

Worksheet 4
Word Search for Older Children

Find the following words in the puzzle and circle them. Words can be up-and-down, horizontal, diagonal, or backwards.

ELIJAH	BULLS	FIRE	JEZREEL	OIL	ZAREPHATH	STICKS
RAVEN	CLOUD	PROPHET	RAIN	DEW	SACRIFICE	KING
WATER	BAAL	AHAB	WIDOW	SON	YAHWEH	FLOUR

```
B A C L E C I F I R C A S O P N W G L M C
A D K U L L O J H B D E L X Q R E Z M L B
H T Y D S T I C K S Q E J E Z R E E L K U
A B G T L O D J I H P M N B F D R E A B L
B A A L B G D R A V E N M H S I D Q P Z L
M A I O U V R U I H K I N G F B J L K U S
H I C F T I O U T E Q P L M J D R A L N S
T O H J I F L O U R P Y E S T Y U M Q O Y
A N O R T V P E P T Y B I R Y P M D N A L
H P U N H R T R C A Z U E Q A P M H G V R
P P N T C E Z A O I L P M U H A U B V X W
E O N T Q A P M B P Y R O V W S T U C E I
R A I N M W Z M I W H V R W E A C L O U D
A S O B E D P T E V L E P X H I W P N A O
Z O M D P W C Y S A W A T E R O P B A Z W
```

Worksheet 5
God Loves Me

Down

1. The Lord will _____ when I call to Him (Psalm 4:3).
3. For God so _____ the world, that He gave His one and only Son (John 3:16).
4. He [God] loved us and sent His _____ (1 John 4:10).
5. You are forgiving and good, O Lord _____ (Psalm 86:5).

Across

2. You are to give him the name _____, because he will save his people from their sins (Matthew 1:21).
4. The Father has sent his Son to be the _____ of the world (1 John 4:14).
6. The Lord is _____ to all (Psalm 145:9).

Worksheet 6
The Flood

God sent a (5)_____ on the earth. God promised to save (8)_____ and his family. God instructed Noah to build an (9)_____.

God told Noah to take his family and (10)_____ of all the animals into the boat. When all were inside, (11)_____ shut the door. The (6)_____ fell for 40 days and nights. When the ark came to rest on a mountain top, Noah sent two birds out in search of dry land.

The (1)_____ never returned.

The (2)_____ brought back an olive (4)_____. After the flood, Noah built an (7)_____ and his family gave thanks. God placed a (3)_____ in the sky as a sign of His promise never again to destroy the world with a flood.

Worksheet 7
What I Do Matters

When God invites you to join Him and you face a crisis of belief, what you do next tells what you believe about God and whether or not you trust Him. What you do reveals what you believe about God regardless of what you say. Wht you believe about God will determine what you do and how you live. Read the following Scriptures and answer the questions.

Matthew 8:5-13
What did the centurion do to demonstrate his faith?

What do you think the centurion believed about Jesus' authority and healing power?

Matthew 8:23-27
What did the disciples do to demonstrate their "little faith" in the middle of this storm?

Matthew 9:20-22
What did the woman do to demonstrate her faith?

What do you think the woman believed about Jesus' power to heal?

Matthew 9:27-31
What trait of God (Jesus) were these two blind men appealing to? (verse 27)

On what basis did Jesus heal these two men? (verse 29)

In closing, how do you show your faith? How do you show you trust God?

Worksheet 8
True Faith Requires Action

Find Hebrews 11 in your Bible. The following list on the left includes people commended for their faith. The verses of the chapter are in parentheses by the name. Match the person on the left with the action on the right that demonstrates faith. Write the correct letters in the blanks.

_____ 1. Abel (verse 4)   A. Chose to be mistreated along with God's people
_____ 2. Enoch (verses 5-6)   B. Offered a righteous sacrifice to God
_____ 3. Noah (verse 7)   C. Made his home in a foreign country
_____ 4. Abraham (verses 8-19)   D. Marched around the walls of Jericho
_____ 5. Joseph (verse 22)   E. Pleased God by earnestly seeking Him
_____ 6. Moses (verses 24-28)   F. Followed God without knowing where he was going.
_____ 7. Israelites (verses 29-30) G. Welcomed and hid the Israelite spies
_____ 8. Rahab (verse 31)   H. Built an ark to save his family

Worksheet 9
Hudson Taylor

Hudson Taylor, a great man of prayer and faith, responded to God's call to go to China as a missionary. His father had already died. He had to leave his widowed mother to go to China. By the end of his life in 1905, he had been used by God to found the China Inland Mission. There were 205 preaching stations, 849 missionaries, and 125,000 Chinese Christians—a testimony of a life absolutely surrendered to God. Hudson Taylor described something of the cost he and his mother experienced as he obeyed God's will to go to China as a missionary.

Imagine that you are Hudson Taylor. Read his account below and answer the questions that follow.

"My beloved, no sainted, mother had come to see me off from Liverpool. Never shall I forget that day, nor how she went with me into the little cabin that was to be my home for nearly six long months. With a mother's loving hand she smoothed the little bed. She sat by my side, and joined me in the last hymn that we should sing together before the long parting. We knelt down, and she prayed the last mother's prayer I was to hear before starting for China. Then notice was given that we must separate, and we had to say good-bye, never expecting to meet on earth again.

"For my sake she restrained her feelings as much as possible. We parted; and she went on shore, giving me her blessing. I stood alone on deck, and she followed the ship as we moved towards the dock gates. As we passed through the gates, and the separation really commenced, I shall never forget the cry of anguish wrung from that mother's heart. It went through me like a knife. I never knew so fully, until then, what 'God so loved the world' meant. And I am quite sure that my precious mother learned more of the love of God to the perishing in that hour than in all her life before.

"Praise God, the number is increasing who are finding out the exceeding joys, the wondrous revelations of His mercies, vouchsafed to those who follow Him, and emptying themselves, leave all in obedience to His great commission."

(Taken from J. Hudson Taylor, *A Retrospect*, Philadelphia: The China Inland Mission, n.d. 39-40)

CW-9

1. What did it cost Hudson Taylor to adjust his life to God and obediently go to China?

2. What did it cost Hudson's mother for him to obey God's will?

3. What did they learn about God's love through this experience?

Leaving home and family on a dangerous mission was a costly step for Hudson Taylor to take. His mother so loved the Lord that she was willing to pay the cost of releasing her son to missions. Both of the Taylors had to pay a high cost for obedience. Yet, they both experienced the love of God in a way they had never known before.

Worksheet 10
People from Our Experiencing God Weekend

Unscramble the letters to form the name of the person from our Experiencing God Weekend.

1. ILJAHE	E _ _ _ _ _	7. SSEMO	M _ _ _ _
2. MDAA	A _ _ _	8. UEMASL	S _ _ _ _ _
3. VEE	E _ _	9. KEHAMSC	M _ _ _ _ _ _
4. HONA	N _ _ _	10. LIHOGAT	G _ _ _ _ _ _
5. LUPA	P _ _ _	11. VADID	D _ _ _ _
6. SESUJ	J _ _ _ _	12. RAAMB	A _ _ _ _ _

Answers to Children's Workbook

Worksheet 1
God Is Always Working

```
C D E M X W V Y O M P F Q T I A Y I E T X U P H M
R W E N B P R E X T I M N W S Q B U A Z N G L P Y
V W A M B A V C X Y A P E S W Z N A M C S T A P I
H T W B I C A Q S P U V W E R X O P B R R P X W K
S Q W T Z I R O D K L T A P N H I X W I N I X S W
Z A V P W A E O P W R Q V A Y P I A D Y N S A A Q
N Y Z A O A A I P N A N E D Q E Z I P A Q T P U B
O Z X V O P Y A A P O T M Q M V W A S D O P I S R
M U C K S O E I P Z X N Q A S G
```

" 'My Father is always at His work to this very day, and I, too, am working' " (John 5:17).

Worksheet 2
Word Match

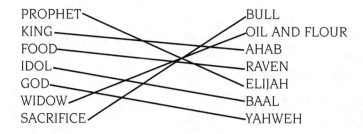

Worksheet 3
Word Search for Younger Children

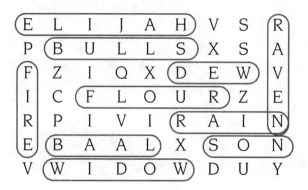

Experiencing God

79

Worksheet 4
Word Search for Older Children

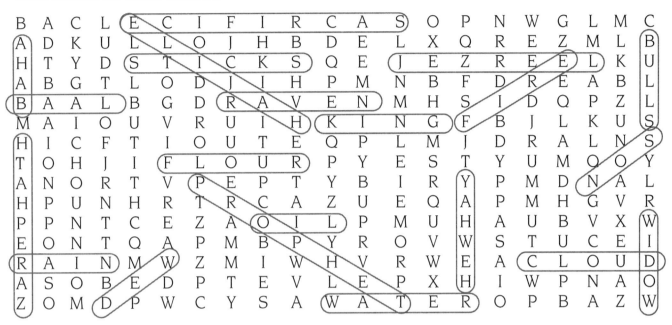

Worksheet 5
God Loves Me

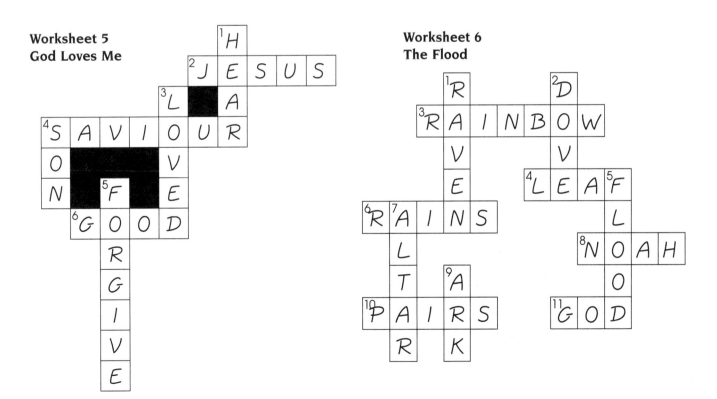

Worksheet 6
The Flood

Worksheet 7
What I Do Matters

Matthew 8:5-13
He asked Jesus to heal his servant without being in the presence of the servant.
The Centurion believed Jesus was under God's authority and that His authority gave Him the power to heal.
Matthew 8:23-27
The disciples panicked during the storm.
Matthew 9:20-22
She sought Jesus and touched the edge of His clothes.
She believed Jesus had the power to heal her.
Matthew 9:27-31
The blind man appealed to Jesus for mercy.
Jesus healed them according to their faith.

Worksheet 8
True Faith Requires Action

    B   1. Abel (verse 4)
    E   2. Enoch (verses 5-6)
    H   3. Noah (verse 7)
    F   4. Abraham (verses 8-19)
    C   5. Joseph (verse 22)
    A   6. Moses (verses 24-28)
    D   7. Israelites (verses 29-30)
    G   8. Rahab (verse 31)

Worksheet 9
Hudson Taylor

1. Hudson had to leave his mother
2. She never saw Hudson again.
3. Hudson and his mother learned that God loved them very much.

Worksheet 10
People from Our Experiencing God Weekend

1. ELIJAH   7. MOSES
2. ADAM   8. SAMUEL
3. EVE   9. MESHACK
4. NOAH   10. GOLIATH
5. PAUL   11. DAVID
6. JESUS   12. ABRAM